Freelance Hairdressing

Fiona Raynes was born in Weymouth and educated at The Royal Alexandra and Albert School, Reigate. She learned the art of hairdressing and beauty at Fareham Tertiary College gaining a distinction in City and Guilds ladies' hairdressing which led her to be one of twelve Hairdresser of the Year finalists. She has entered, won and judged various hairdressing competitions. From the age of eighteen she owned her own salon and ran it successfully for six years. Altogether she has worked in six different hairdressing salons.

Whilst bringing up her family Fiona Raynes was a freelance hairdresser for fourteen years, and enjoyed the flexibility it offered. Fiona has worked in a variety of places and achieved, on each occasion, a full client base and service range within three months.

In the past she has taught hairdressing, art and associated subjects at Fareham Tertiary College and, currently, she is working part-time at MDS Training and Management Consultants, Weymouth, as a hairdressing lecturer teaching NVQ hairdressing. She is a member of the Freelance Hair and Beauty Federation. One of her interests is helping the Weymouth Drama Group with their productions producing different historical hairstyles and make-up effects. She is married with three children and lives in Weymouth.

Freelance Hairdressing

A Guide

ISBN 0 7090 6029 7

Robert Hale Limited
Clerkenwell House
Clerkenwell Green
London EC1R 0HT

2   4   6   8   10   9   7   5   3   1

Photoset in North Wales by
Derek Doyle & Associates, Mold, Clwyd.
Printed in Great Britain by
St Edmundsbury Press Ltd, Bury St Edmunds, Suffolk.
Bound by WBC Book Manufacturers Limited,
Bridgend, Mid-Glamorgan.

Contents

Introduction

Whilst knowledge of the history of hairdressing is certainly not essential, it is worth recalling that the care and arrangement of the hair have been of considerable social significance since earliest times. Even amongst the most primitive tribes and in ancient Egypt and Assyria, elaborate hairstyles were commonplace and for centuries age, rank, political allegiance, marital status, etc. have all played their part in dictating how the hair should be arranged.

However, for the present purpose, one needs go back no further than 1882 when the Incorporated Guild of Hairdressers, Wigmakers and Perfumers was set up. Membership was open to master hairdressers, proprietors of salons and manufacturers and wholesalers of hairdressing products, every applicant had to be proposed and seconded by a guild member (usually a man), and all premises were inspected for suitability.

Then, in 1942, the National Hairdressers' Federation was founded with membership confined to master hairdressers and those whose livelihood was dependent on the ownership and control of a hairdressing establishment. Excluded were manufacturers, suppliers and employees. A fundamental issue was the protection of the trade from unqualified hairdressers and provision was also made for technical classes for apprentices.

After the Second World War hairdressing courses were introduced at technical colleges but there was still resistance amongst hairdressers to those who had been trained only in that manner. It was then that fully qualified hairdressers who were offered only junior positions in salons found the option of going freelance very attractive. A further inducement was the 1980s Enterprise Allowance Scheme, which offered free management training and £40 a week for a year. Self-employment was further encouraged by salon owners themselves who, as a result of the recession in the late 1980s, offered hairdressers the chance to become self-employed by means of the 'rent-a-chair' system.

Finally, in 1993, the Freelance Hair and Beauty Federation was founded and so began an era when, recognized standards having been achieved, the freelance became generally accepted.

Freelance hairdressing is the way forward – the future of hairdressing. It is a personal service in which the customer's satisfaction is the key to success. Having one's hair cut is a frequent occurrence and clients usually like to have the same hairdresser; as a freelance hairdresser one can offer a more flexible service than a salon and at a reasonable price. There is a growing market for this service, comprising those unable or unwilling to go to a salon, such as mothers with young children, people who have no spare time during 'salon hours' and the housebound. Salons may see this growth as a threat and claim a lack of standards and professionalism amongst freelance hairdressers. However, I believe there is a place for both salon and freelance hairdressing.

Freelance hairdressing is an interesting career because it offers the operator freedom, identity, friendship and status. It gives an individual the opportunity to be creative, providing not only financial rewards but also that feeling of pride when you say goodbye to another satisfied customer.

Traditionally hairdressers are not highly paid. Why, after a training period that lasts at least three years, does a hairdresser not deserve more? A freelance has a real chance of achieving a worthwhile income. The entrepreneur will find that setting up independently of the salon is financially viable since hairdressing is not very capital-intensive. Even if one does not have much capital it is possible to set up in business with just scissors and comb in this age of easy 'wash and wear' styles. Over a period one can build up to the full range of services, such as setting, blow-drying, perming and colouring, with each new client being your walking advert. After only a short time the client base should be large enough to fulfil personal earnings targets.

The client needs an accessible, friendly hairdresser with whom communication is quick and effective so that any problems can be solved together. Then, too, there is the matter of fitting in appointments between commitments such as the client's own job, childcare, etc. Many working people find it hard to fit hair appointments into the working day and it is during their leisure hours that it is perhaps more convenient and relaxing to have their hair styled. This is where the freelance hairdresser is at a premium. Visiting relaxed clients in their homes makes business a pleasure for all concerned.

Customer service and flexibility are the keywords for the nineties. 'Spending' times are completely different from just twenty years ago; then it was accepted that a nine-to-five job was the norm and one could look forward to Sundays off, and that if you had not finished your shopping by 5.30 on Saturday you would have to wait until Monday morning when the shops reopened. Today, however, we have late-night shopping, with a flexible workforce fitting into the new 24-hour spending opportunity. The personal service sector in particular is expanding, with a growing demand for health and beauty services.

There is plenty of scope here for the hairdressing and beauty entrepreneur to offer a personal service that is flexible enough to meet clients' changing needs; larger organizations may find it hard to compete. A salon's high overheads are often blamed for the low-paid nature of this labour-intensive job but a solution to this problem is to keep expendable costs low; cut out rent and electricity bills, and increase profits for the operator. Freelance hairdressing, therefore, has to be the way forward for those who want to get ahead.

In the final analysis it can be seen that, through changes cultural, political, social and technological, the hairdressing industry is reacting to new demands from those who really matter, the clients, who will only accept and pay for a service that meets their requirements.

In conclusion, I hope this book will answer every question posed by budding freelance hairdressers, by those who are looking at hairdressing as a new career option and by those who have already trained and want to run a business successfully and to achieve a fulfilling career.

1 Basic Requirements and Training

To be successful as a freelance hairdresser, i.e. a hairdresser who works independently of a salon, one must possess certain hairdressing qualifications, business skills, personal attributes, artistic flair and flexibility.

In the first instance a sound technical training is essential. This is gained in further education colleges or in local training agencies offering either full-time or part-time courses over a three year period. Another option is to learn full-time at a private hairdressing school where the courses are usually for six months or a year. Whichever option you choose, you will have to make sure you are happy with the quality of the training offered.

In the past the City and Guilds basic and advanced hairdressing qualifications were the certificates being studied countrywide. However, City and Guilds got together with the Hairdressing Training Board and developed the National Vocational Qualification. NVQ courses are more flexible because in theory you can join them at any time (rather than waiting until the former customary September starting date) and study each unit as it becomes available.

NVQ level 2 in Hairdressing

The full level 2 certificate consists of eleven units, as follows:

1. Reception
2. Consultation and diagnosis
3. Shampooing
4. Conditioning
5. Cutting
6. Blow-drying
7. Setting
8. Permanent waving
9. Colouring
10. Neutralizing
11. Selling

As of 1 September 1996, the cost of such a course at a further education college is around £370.30 (or £277.80 with tax relief) for enrolment and £25.95 (or £19.46 with tax relief) for registration. Each unit costs £2.30, making a total cost of £25.30 (or £18.97 with tax relief).

NVQ level 3 in Hairdressing

NVQ level 3 consists of sixteen units and concentrates on teaching management skills and advanced hairdressing techniques. It trains students to:

1. Contribute to the development of teams and individuals to enhance performance.
2. Assess candidate performance.
3. Contribute to the planning, allocation and supervision of work.
4. Maintain stock control procedures to fulfil operational requirements.
5. Create, maintain and enhance productive working relationships.
6. Maintain healthy, safe and secure working conditions.
7. Provide advice and maintain and provide information for action towards organizations' objectives within given area of responsibility.

8. Establish and maintain effective relationships with clients.
9. Monitor and maintain the receipt of payments from clients for the purchase of goods and services.
10. Contribute to the promotion of hairdressing services and systems.
11. Contribute to the improvement of services and systems.
12. Monitor and maintain client consultation and procedures.
13. Cut hair using specialist cutting techniques.
14. Change the degree of movement and direction of hair by permanent means.
15. Dress hair to produce a specialized range of effects.
16. Create a range of effects using specialist colouring techniques.

The cost of such a course at a further education college would be around £114.00 (or £86.64 with tax relief) if undertaken part-time (four hours per week). It is free for full-time students aged sixteen to eighteen; fees for those over nineteen are subject to status. The registration fee is £42 (or £31.50 with tax relief). Each unit costs £2.10, making a total cost of £33.60 (or £25.20 with tax relief).

Highly desirable, too, is an NVQ level 3 course in Beauty Therapy. This will be beneficial in the long run because you can then offer more services to your clients, boosting profits and making your job more varied and interesting. Once again this subject can be studied part-time or full-time at a further education college, training agency or private school. Students learn how to:

1. Maintain employment standards.
2. Support a healthy, safe and secure salon environment.
3. Liaise with clients and colleagues.
4. Undertake salon reception duties.
5. Provide a service to the customer.
6. Process a sale.

7. Achieve a sale.
8. Deal with returned goods and complaints.
9. Apply and instruct on make-up.
10. Provide lash and brow treatments.
11. Provide and deal with nail care.
12. Provide depilatory waxing.
13. Pierce ears.

One three-hour session a week for three years works out at £85.50 per year, while two sessions a week for two years will cost £171 per year. All the course details will vary between training centres. Telephone or write to your local centres for more information.

These qualifications achieved, you will still have limited experience despite having worked for a year in the salon. You will be learning continuously as you go along, both technically and practically, as well as gaining logistical and organizational skills. In fact in hairdressing you are learning something new constantly, even when you are experienced, because everyone's hair is different. You could start by doing all your friends' and family's hair, building up your clientele from there, and perhaps specializing in up-to-the-minute fashion styles and techniques.

If you are unsure about going freelance, it may be worth working a little longer in a salon until you feel more confident in yourself. When you are freelance, you do not have the support or benefit of other hairdressers in the same room as yourself whose advice you can seek. However, if you have a problem whilst you are visiting a client, then the support available to you will be over the telephone, from either main retailers such as Wella or your local hairdressing supplies wholesaler; they may have a hairdresser working for them who can help.

If you have no constraints such as children, then you are in a very good position to offer a completely flexible approach to your clients' needs, perhaps starting early in the mornings or working later into the evening.

If you are a fully qualified and experienced hairdresser,

you can choose to work with whichever kind of client you prefer or to specialize in a particular skill, for example cutting and perming. With your experience you will be able to offer all the services and enjoy the benefits of being a business owner; this book will give you ideas to improve your long-term career plan and profit.

If you are returning to hairdressing after a break away to have your family, you are in a very fortunate position, although it may be worth updating your skills. Your local further education college or training centre will be able to help you in this respect. To start with, your working speed may be a little slower than it used to be, but very soon you will find that you are back up to par and will feel you have never been away. Once you have learned all your basic skills you never forget them.

Male freelance hairdressers are currently in the minority, though they could be very successful either as specialist barbers or unisex hairdressers. A freelance barber would be useful to businessmen who do not have time to get to a salon in their free time and could be visited in the office during a break – or to those gents who would prefer a confidential toupee fitting. Some ladies prefer to have a man style their hair; from a safety point of view, as housewives invite repairmen into their home who carry out their business professionally, why not a hairdresser?

Working for yourself, as with all things, has advantages and disadvantages. The advantages are that you will not be bound by salon rules, you have control over the products you use, you can plan and use your time more effectively, you can earn more, tax is in your favour for items you use (for example, your car) and you have very low overheads with no rent to pay.

The disadvantages are potentially longer working hours, having to record all financial transactions, the valuable time it takes to travel to clients and of course the fact that you are responsible for all the work you have done. As you can see, there are more advantages than disadvantages when you work for yourself.

15

In addition to the above basic requirements, other personal qualities are needed if you want to be successful, for example being professional and businesslike. Your personality and appearance are probably the two most important aspects which clients will notice about you first. Being pleasant, considerate and helpful all day can be hard work for some, but they are abilities you must be able to demonstrate every day at any time, even if you are telephoned at 10 p.m. by a demanding client!

A positive attitude and a willingness to listen to your client are essential when you are running your own business. Most clients enjoy talking and need to be listened to sympathetically. The skill of listening and knowing when to give your opinion is very important. You need to like meeting different people and to be able to deal with all kinds of situations in a professional manner, putting clients at ease so you can communicate effectively. You may have children as part of your clientele and they will need the same level of care and understanding you give to their mums and dads.

Hairdressing is a physically demanding job. Your personal fitness and stamina need to be considered when you are likely to be on your feet all day. These factors will be even more important if you are planning to walk or cycle to your clients' houses. Wear comfortable clothes and footwear and ensure you have regular sit-down breaks. Enjoy the feeling of well-being when you start freelance hairdressing this way.

If you have a car, then rests are built into your busy days, but it is important to keep fit by exercising your whole body as well. One way to keep fit anywhere, even in your car whilst driving or when you have a few minutes spare, is by using isometric exercises. Such exercises will keep you supple and feeling relaxed. The principle is simple: any muscle is contracted through pushing, pulling, squeezing or pressing against an immovable object, making your muscles work hard and promoting strength, tone and endurance. Just tense your muscles or push against something to the count of ten, relax and repeat four times or until you feel tired. Other effective ways of exercising are dancing, walking, aerobics, cycling and swimming.

When you are working, think about your posture and correct it if you feel you are putting unnecessary strain on your back. The human backbone is naturally curved in an 'S' shape. Do not stand ramrod straight, but always relax your shoulders and keep your torso comfortably erect, hips steady, stomach tucked in. Ask your client to sit on a lower or higher chair if it feels better for you. When picking up your hairdressing equipment or a child, always remember to bend your knees, keeping your spine straight. Never stoop as you will put undue strain on your back.

Punctuality is something your clients will expect, especially if they are busy people with other commitments in their lives. Being punctual will also help your time management. Sometimes, due to circumstances beyond your control, it is not possible to be on time and it is then necessary to warn your client of any delay. Organization is the key to successful time management.

Your ability and artistic flair are also extremely important. As you can see from the courses available, all the information and training you acquire will give clients confidence and respect for your opinion. Equally, being qualified will give you as a hairdresser self-confidence. This will help clients to relax in your company and trust in your experienced judgement and advice. Being able to keep cool in an emergency is another attribute you will need to have. Your ability has to stand out against your competitors and this can only be achieved by giving your clients, as individuals, the styles they really want, ranging from the conventional to the highly creative. It is difficult to be creative when you are tired, so ensure that you work sensible hours – for your and your clients' benefit.

Support from your family and friends is an aspect which is not always considered fully. A business can be a very time-consuming occupation, especially when it starts to take off. It is important from the outset for you to know what your business commitment is and to tell your family and friends. They need to know because the business will touch all their lives, for example when clients ring up for

17

appointments or when you may have to ask for help with your own childcare arrangements. If initial expectations change and exceed original plans, ensure that all those who support you understand and can still help you.

Flexibility is the whole essence of freelance hairdressing. In order to be fully flexible you must always be positive, be able to solve problems on an ongoing basis, share information, be self-disciplined with a passion for your business and believe in what you are doing.

You will be able to become a freelance hairdresser if you have the necessary skills and the ability to sell yourself, but you will need to find out more. This book will help you start and run a successful business by giving you lots of good ideas, from promotion to keeping your hard-won clients. Many people just like you have succeeded in the exciting endeavour of starting their own business.

It is vital that you consider all commercial as well as creative aspects of your business. Within your job you will be wearing many different 'hats', you will be serving both your clients' and your own long-term interests. Your personal goals must be analysed, including any training requirements needed to achieve them, the welfare and safety of yourself and clients, your business image, growth and development.

Once you start working for yourself it is important to know what you want to achieve and to have clear goals to aim at, in other words develop a personal career structure and identify opportunities for advancement. Most of the areas you will need to consider are covered in this book, but if you need practical experience it is worth joining a group of students on a course. By training and taking courses which interest you, you can improve your business knowledge and be more aware of chances which can be pursued, enabling you to perform better, to increase care for your clients or to make more money. Here are some suggested courses which could help:

Practical bookkeeping – this will give you more confidence in your accounting skills. Looking at all financial aspects to do with your business, it gives you an advantage when filling out tax returns and saves accountancy fees.

Business studies – this will give you a broad view of how business operates in the UK and in Europe.

Car maintenance – be independent whilst on the road and help yourself! This course will help you with basic car maintenance.

Self-defence – you may feel this is an option worth pursuing, especially when you are out and about on your own.

Keep fit – look good and feel great. Keep fit classes will build your energy levels and help you through busy days – and they are good for reducing stress too.

First-aid – a practical course which will help you to remember first-aid procedures.

Photography – learn to take excellent photographs of your work to sell back to clients or promote your business through your style book.

Psychology – this will help you to understand where people are 'coming from', perhaps enabling you to communicate more effectively.

Assertiveness training – a useful skill when running a business. Find out how to have the power to make choices and be your own person.

Managing time – time is a most precious resource and cannot be replaced. Learn how to manage *it* rather than *it* managing *you*.

Coping with stress – learn about techniques to reduce stress in your life.

Selling skills – this is a practical subject and you may need more experience.

Motivate yourself by setting your own goals. When you achieve them, reward yourself; for example, a target could be dealing with your fiftieth client or gaining access to a large firm that requires your services. Reward yourself by giving yourself a present, maybe having a day off, buying a new outfit or getting your hair done! You are special – don't forget it.

Look after yourself whilst getting to work, and when you

get there. Keep away from potentially dangerous places, such as built-up areas in towns and cities after dark where you may be at risk from undesirable personalities or gangs. Make sure whatever mode of transport you choose is reliable and will get you home. If you have a car, join the RAC (Royal Automobile Club), AA (Automobile Association) or other similar rescue organization. Take a mobile phone if you have one, or carry a phonecard or change to make a call from a phone box.

Once at work protect yourself from your hairdressing products by wearing suitable protection, overalls and rubber or plastic gloves. Open windows to ventilate the room you are working in if you are perming or colouring hair. Your hands need extra special care so use a barrier cream or hand cream. If your hands are sore you will not be able to work effectively, if at all.

Another safety net you can put into place is an insurance policy that covers you financially if you need to take time away from work due to sickness or disability. Shop around the various insurance companies and ensure you get the right amount of cover.

Interpersonal relationships should be developed and used to communicate effectively not only with your clients but with all your other business contacts too. This usually means that you will be doing a lot more listening than talking.

When you are working for yourself you may experience feelings of isolation, especially from other hairdressers. Try building up a network by contacting other freelance stylists in your area; it is important that you do not feel isolated as this will demotivate you.

Second only to hairdressing experience is the need for a sound commercial approach towards the whole enterprise and this is dealt with in detail in Chapter 3.

2　Getting Started

Getting started in business is probably the most difficult step to take for three main reasons; if you have never been self-employed, are new to an area and do not know anyone, or live in an area where there are other hairdressers who offer the same or a similar service, you may be wondering how to start and get yourself noticed ahead of the competition. The most important attribute you should possess at this point is confidence that your business will succeed, because without this self-belief you are more likely to fail.

Renting a chair

If you are not quite confident enough to go into business alone, becoming self-employed may be easier than you think because as a hairdresser you can do this with little risk by renting a chair from a salon. The advantages of doing this are that you will be operating in an already established salon with other experienced stylists who will be able to give you their advice about hairdressing and keeping accurate records for tax purposes. There should be no reason for you to do any market research since the advert in the paper for another hairdresser is usually in response to a growing demand from clients in the salon. Other advantages include the availability of a part-time or full-time receptionist, who can take calls and make appointments for stylists, and a cupboard in which to store your equipment and stock.

Adverts for renting chairs in salons come up from time to time and are usually found in the local press, with a telephone number to ring for details. The person you will be contacting will be the salon owner or manager, who will not only give information about requirements but ask questions too. Before telephoning, prepare a list of things you would like to know about and think about responses you may have to give to questions, such as how much experience you have, how many hours you intend to work, etc. You will also want to ask what you can expect in terms of business and why the salon is renting a chair.

Salon managers are looking for hairdressers who are able to cover the chair-renting cost every week. The initial interview on the telephone should inform you where the salon is, what the salon will provide and the cost of chair-renting. From this conversation, if there is mutual interest, then an appointment date and time for an interview will be set.

If there is competition from other hairdressers to rent a chair in a particular salon, especially if it has a good reputation with clients and is located in a lucrative area, a curriculum vitae (c.v.) may be requested in order for the manager to ascertain who is most suitable to meet the demand. A c.v. in this instance should show your ability to build up a clientele quickly and to keep written records of takings. An example of how a c.v. could be set out can be found in Appendix 2.

After sending a c.v. (if one was asked for), you will hopefully be requested to attend an interview of a practical nature where a demonstration of your skills is observed. When the interview is arranged, ask what you will be demonstrating to ensure you take the correct equipment and stock with you. The manager usually provides a 'client' for you. Details of your past hairdressing experience will be requested along with evidence that you are willing to be self-employed and able to keep all your own business records. Information on how to keep financial records can be found in Chapters 3 and 4.

Preparation before an interview is essential. Beforehand, try and guess which questions the interviewer may ask so you can reply confidently. Here are some potential questions:

- 'I see from your c.v. that you built up a clientele in six months. Can you tell me what kind of client you are attracting?'
- 'Do you have any queries about being self-employed?'
- 'How many hours are you planning to work and when?'
- 'Are you confident that you will be able to cover the renting cost every week?'

Plan your travel arrangements to make sure you know where the salon is located and how long it takes to get there. Ensure you arrive at your destination in good time (preferably arrive at least five minutes before the interview), looking calm, collected and smart. When choosing an outfit, if you have the opportunity go and see what existing team members of the salon are wearing and select something similar.

Interviews are a two-way process, and if you are accepted on to the salon team, you need to know exactly where you stand in all aspects of the business before an agreement can be reached by you and the manager. Issues to be discussed will include:

- Charges for full-time or part-time renting, when the money is due, what exactly you are getting for your money and whether there are any hidden or unexpected costs.
- The contract's length and the period of notice required if either party wishes to terminate it.
- Uniform requirements (if any), provision of equipment and stock and storage arrangements for it.
- Your status – whether or not you are classed as 'free-lance'; for example, can you work in other salons or places as you wish? (If you plan to work elsewhere, a liability insurance policy will need to be taken out.)

When all aspects have been discussed and an agreement reached, it must be written down and signed by both parties. All salon owners who operate a rent-a-chair system run it differently, depending on their expectations and existing set-up. To rent a chair full-time costs from £50 upwards per week in an out-of-town salon. Included in this will be the cost of electricity and perhaps use of towels; everything else is usually extra.

As soon as you start to rent your chair, remember to contact your local tax office and the social security office, who need to know your status for National Insurance contribution purposes. Both offices will give very helpful advice and support.

Going freelance

If becoming self-employed via the chair-renting route does not sound appealing, given below are summarized guidelines of the preparation that needs to be done before one can confidently start in business as a sole trader.

Market research

Market research is the first stage of your preparation. This is where you assess if it is worth starting a business in the area of your choice or at a certain location, for example old people's homes. You must analyse the competition and find out if some service could be offered which is currently lacking. A thorough knowledge of your potential clients is essential and so too is the overall business image required to attract them. For more details of market research see Chapter 2.

Insurance

Liability insurance is a necessity regardless of how many hours you hope to work. Obtain at least three quotes and ensure the policy you choose gives adequate cover for any claim you may need to submit in the future. Liability insurance usually covers damage to your clients and their property up to the value of £1 million. Ask your local insurance company for details of extra cover available. Some companies will allow you to spread the cost of the policy and pay it off in instalments over a period of one year.

A starting date

Choose the actual day on which you want to start trading. This will give you a deadline to work to, ensuring you complete all business preparation beforehand. You will need to open a bank account, find out if you are eligible for a business grant, inform the local council of your intention to trade (because you may have to be registered) and finally contact your local tax and social security offices (for the purpose of National Insurance payments), informing them of your start date. It is always a good idea to give yourself deadlines in all aspects of your business because this will help you to be more focused and achieve your goals.

A business plan

Your business plan is the culmination of your market research, timings and financial planning. It organizes and pulls together your business aims in one document and is essential for two reasons: to present for your own benefit your commercial intentions and expectations over your first year of trading, enabling you to plan ahead; and, if necessary, to persuade your bank manager to lend you money or provide an overdraft facility.

Stock purchase

Using the information from the business plan, some stock and equipment may have to be purchased so you are ready on your first day. Finally, about one week before the business start date, advertisements should be put in local shop windows and the local newspaper. Thorough preparation is the key to a successful business.

Location

Consider the area you wish to trade in, whether it is a village, town or city, and the various strategies which should be adopted when dealing with these different locations.

Starting business in a village

If you want to work in and around a village, you will be entering a close-knit community where most people know each other. What you need most in this instance is personal recommendation. News of your arrival will travel fast and you want it to be good! If you have a bad first review, it is like a kiss of death and potential clients will be reluctant to come forward from that moment onward.

Imagine that you have to go through a series of 'gates' before you are fully accepted into the village scene and that at each gate there is a 'gatekeeper', who will either let you in or block you. If you really do not know anyone else, then start by getting to know the proprietor of the local newsagents, who will have extensive knowledge of the village and the people who live there. This person will have a certain amount of influence and their opinion will probably be respected by the other villagers. In effect, this is your first interview so pick a quiet time when you have the opportunity to chat and create a good impression. Your mission is to place your beautifully presented advertising card in the shop window and thus promote your business via the first gatekeeper of the village – the newsagent. Dress in a smart but casual way and make sure your hair and make-up are perfect. Before you enter the shop you will probably feel nervous, so prepare in your own mind what you want to say and any questions you wish to ask. You need to find out if there are any other freelance hairdressers in the area, how long they have been operating and the services they offer. Quite often there are 'invisible' hairdressers around who do not need to advertise because they are well known and have been in the area for a long time.

When you enter the shop, smile and explain who you are and what you aim to do. Listen to what the 'interviewer' is saying. Do not appear to be pushy; remember, you are trying to create a good first impression so that the newsagent tells customers about the friendly new hairdresser in the area. Treat everyone you meet as though they are potential clients. Your open, pleasant approach will soon make you many new acquaintances. Your card will reflect your image; backed up with a small advert in the local free paper, it will alert potential clients to your existence. This approach may be enough for you to get your first crucial client, and once potential clients can see how good you are it will not take long before your appointment book is full.

Alternatively, if your business does not seem to be taking off as quickly as you would like, then try this approach. Carry on placing your advertising card in the local newsagent and backing it up with an advert in the paper, but ask around to see if there are any craft fairs, table sales, fêtes, etc. and book space. If you are feeling generous, offer to give a percentage of your profit to the fund-raisers too – this gesture will help you in the long run. Set up your stall as described in Chapter 8 and aim to attract mainly children to start with, by perhaps displaying photographs of famous footballers and pop stars or even by having toys for them to play with! Children are excellent first clients; once they have had their hair cut, their parents will usually follow. Ensure also that your portfolio of photographs is available, so that as much positive information about you as possible can be scrutinized whilst you are working. Promote hair parties so that you can get to know small groups of friends and gradually widen your circle of clients. Do not forget to leave a pile of business cards so that potential clients can take one and make sure you are easy to get hold of; it is very frustrating for clients who cannot communicate with you very quickly.

If there happens to be competition from other

hairdressers, do not be put off. Competition is healthy because it keeps standards high. Give a better service by offering excellent client care and special products that are exclusive to you. Listen to and provide what your clients want. There is always a small percentage of clients who drift from one hairdresser to another, staying for a while before moving on to try someone new. These experienced clients are good to have, especially if they like you, because they will appreciate what you are doing and will want to tell all their friends. Some of those potential clients who try you will hopefully become loyal to you in the long term.

Once you have managed to get yourself into the village scene and have gained the trust of your clients, protect yourself by keeping standards high *every* time you style their hair. If you start sending greetings cards for special occasions, keep up the habit and ensure that any promises and undertakings to clients are realistic and are honoured.

Starting business in a town

In many ways, starting business in a town is similar to work in a village because a town is made up of many small communities all linked together by families, education centres, social clubs, old folks' homes, hospitals, work contacts, etc. Once again, the task is to find the influential gatekeepers who will allow you access to the clients you would like to work for. As in a village, post advertising cards around your chosen area, in newsagents, etc. and endeavour to publicly demonstrate your skills.

When writing your small advert for the personal column in the local paper, specify the area or district you are willing to visit. If this is not done, you may be asked to travel miles away from where you live and this will not be cost-effective – all your profit will go on petrol. When choosing the size of area you wish to cover, bear in mind the distance and amount of time it takes to travel from one side of it to another. If you are in any doubt about timings, try routes you are likely to take at different times of the day. You will very quickly become familiar with the area this way too.

Because towns are larger you will be able to specialize, as there are more people requiring a similar service. If wedding work is what you wish to concentrate on, ensure that you attend wedding fairs; these tend to be held in springtime and brides-to-be may want to book you well in advance for the current year and beyond. In this way you can plan and commit yourself in the long term to your business.

Starting business in a city
There are usually two main parts to a city, business and residential. Decide which part you would like to work in and access the 'gatekeeper' – the individual who knows the area and holds the keys to your acceptance into the community. You may intend to combine both sectors. In the business part, because of the changing employment market, large companies are keen to attract and keep key, quality staff and one way they have found to to this is to offer their staff access to gym facilities and beauty services; therefore a freelance hairdresser and/or beauty therapist would be very welcome in some firms.

Approach firms with a well-planned 'package' of what you can offer to staff and outline the overall benefits to the company. Here is an example of how you can sell your idea:

- Find out whether the firm has a hairdresser or beautician. If it does not, contact the personnel or human resources manager and make an appointment to see them.
- Prepare a very smart, word-processed document you can leave with the manager. The document should reflect the image you are projecting via colour scheme, layout and typeface, and it should begin with an introduction outlining the benefits to the company of your skills. Two examples include convenience for staff and an opportunity for them to relax, which in turn will help to produce better workers for the company. A list of services offered and price list should also be included and don't forget to mention your qualifications.

- Propose frequency and timings of visits – this aspect will be negotiable.
- Find out where you will be able to operate from. Is there a room you can use? What facilities are available?
- Work out how you expect to be paid. You could be subsidized by the company, or paid via normal charges made direct to staff.

When you are working for a company, staff will generally only have time for a haircut. As each staff member will have to go back to work, make a special effort to protect clothing with gowns and remove all cut hair from the client's face and neck.

If you decide to work in the residential part of a city, the principles are the same as for starting business in a town. One big difference may be the type of housing you will have to visit to get to clients, namely blocks of flats. Be prepared to climb many stairs if lifts are out of order and use a rucksack for your equipment.

Whether you are going to work in a village, town or city, two issues apply to all areas: they concern your own safety and the security of your stock and equipment. Do not visit any area where you fear for your personal safety and if you absolutely have to keep any stock or equipment in your car that is not required immediately, it should be locked out of sight in the boot of your car.

3 A Commercial Approach to Freelance Hairdressing

Having established that you have the necessary qualifications and personal attributes to become a successful freelance hairdresser, the first step is to undertake some research to establish that a market exists for your services in your chosen area. This is essential to avoid failure at the outset. Start by looking in the local newspapers, newsagents' windows and by asking around. Find out exactly who and what your competition is, i.e. other freelance hairdressers, beauticians, salons and shops that sell beauty products (if you decide to sell products too).

The number of potential clients in your area is also important: there must be enough to support your business. If you live in a large village, town or city there will probably be sufficient within a fairly small area, but if you live in the countryside you must be prepared to travel further.

Potential clients can be men, women and children in their homes or in such varied places as schools, hospitals, old people's homes, performing groups, playgroups, large companies, etc. Weddings are worth investigating, although this can be seasonal work. You could also specialize in groups who have their own methods of styling hair. More details can be found in Chapter 6.

Market research

Market research is usually carried out by devising a short

questionnaire asking a sample of people what they think about your business idea. Obviously, the more people you ask the more precise the result will be. However, to be practical, if you hope to go full-time ask between approximately twenty-five to seventy-five people to ascertain whether your idea is popular or not and fewer if you plan to go part-time. Preferably the results should be collected personally, either by knocking on doors (cold calling) or by standing in a busy street to catch passers-by. Talking direct to the type of client you want to work for gives feedback which is more valid; for example, if you want to work with families, ask parents whilst they are waiting to pick their children up from school. Another advantage of using the personal approach is that this is the first point of contact with potential clients and is a good public relations exercise. When asking questions choose a time when the weather is mild and dry; people are not going to be inclined to answer questions in the pouring rain.

Remember that your business idea is only a means of solving a problem for your clients. People will be interested in your business not merely because it is a wonderful idea but because it gives them the opportunity to have their hair styled as they want it, at a convenient time and at a fair price. Here are some examples of queries you could put in your questionnaire:

- What problems do you and your family have when you want to have your hair styled?
- How are you overcoming the problems at present? (Or how would you overcome them?)
- How satisfied are you with the results?
- What other ways of having your hair styled do you know about?
- How would you react to having your own personal hairdresser, who would visit you in your home or at work at your convenience?
- What sort of price do you think would be realistic for such a service?

- Would you consider using such a service yourself?

Getting people to talk about the issue will be far more useful to you (and a future financial backer) than asking detailed questions about irrelevant business matters. Once you are satisfied with the result of your market research and you have established that there is a local demand for your services, the next step is to plan your price list.

Establishing a price list

It is essential to formulate your price list correctly at the outset because if you charge too little you may be unable to achieve acceptable profits – and it will be more difficult to put your prices up later. Your market research will give you a good indication of what people generally expect to pay. You may win extra trade by charging low prices, but on the whole price-cutting is not the best way to develop a business. Alternatively, if you charge too much you may only obtain a small clientele. Of course, some clients may prefer to spend more, thinking they are getting a superior service. It is better to aim for a high-quality service and to charge a fair price.

See how much the competition is charging so that you get an idea of the acceptable price range. However, you must ensure your charges cover your costs and provide a worthwhile net income. The business plan (see Appendix 1) will show you what your charge per hour needs to be. If, for example, it works out at £10 an hour, then it would not be unreasonable to charge £5 for a haircut, £10 for a cut and blow-dry and £20 for a perm.

Some hairdressers charge what they feel they are worth. This may stem from charges made in salons where they worked. Prices across the country do not reflect the general north–south trading pattern. Rather it is that city charges are the highest, followed by town and country. London is possibly the most expensive city.

If you do not have all the equipment, stock or transport you need to start in business nor the money to fund it, you will have to borrow. Your local Training and Enterprise Council will direct you to organizations that may be able to give you a grant. If you are under thirty, the Prince's Youth Business Trust may be worth contacting. Your Business Link or the Department of Trade and Industry (DTI) can be of help. If you need to approach a bank, you must convince the manager that he will get his money back and this almost certainly entails producing a business plan.

You will need to open a bank account and it is worth shopping around for the best deal, which may include free banking for a year or lower interest rates. Some banks produce free information for those starting in business. The convenience factor must also be taken into account in making your choice of bank. Potentially the most expensive item you will need to purchase is transport but this can be delayed if you decide to follow the shoestring budget outlined below, in which case no financing will be necessary.

Even if you do not need to borrow money, it is still a good idea to produce a business plan because it will help you to define your goals and keep you on track to a profitable business. A business plan explains exactly what your business will do, where you will operate and who your planned customers are. It also summarizes your forecasts for the business for one year. It is inadvisable to try and predict further ahead because your figures will not be accurate enough. The length of the plan should only be about two or three pages plus the financial forecasts. Financiers will assume that if your presentation to them is unsatisfactory, your presentation to customers will be equally unsatisfactory, so produce it in a readable form, neatly typed and in a smart folder.

The business plan includes all likely expenditure necessary to offer a complete service. However, it is entirely possible to commence trading on a shoestring. It is possible to produce first-rate haircuts by cutting hair dry or by wetting it down with water rather than washing it. In this case, all you really need are the following:

	£
A pair of hairdressing scissors	7.00
A comb	1.00
A gown for your client	10.00 (half if you make your own)
Liability insurance	60.00 (which can be paid in instalments)
	———
TOTAL	78.00

As you make more money, you can add more services to your list and gradually build up your equipment and stock to the levels shown in the business plan. Your first, most important acquisition will be a vehicle so that you can satisfy customers who cannot easily be reached by foot or public transport.

Although £78 will get you started, your basic stock will not cost much less than £200. The following are the major items and, as a matter of interest, I compare wholesale and high street prices (September 1995), which show little superficial difference. However, professional perms and tints are stronger and give better results in the hands of the professional. Another advantage of dealing with a wholesaler is its convenience – orders can be made over the telephone and goods can be delivered direct to your door. You may also be able to negotiate credit terms or get a discount by buying in bulk.

You will also need to take into account a modicum of advertising (perhaps £40, which is enough to cover three months of advertising in the personal column of the local newspaper and the cost of placing cards in newsagents' windows) and public transport fares.

Another promotional option is to put advertising on your car. A sign with your business name and telephone number in your business colours looks very professional. Three signs can be fixed, one on each of the two front doors and, if there

ITEM	WHOLESALER £	HIGH STREET CHEMIST £
Scissors	17.63	6.00
Comb	1.18	1.00
Brush	4.70	4.15
Hairdryer	22.32	30.00
Gown	11.75	5.00
Ten towels	15.28	30.00
Tongs	7.05	9.00
Shampoo 4.5 l.	5.88	5.00
Conditioner 4.5 l.	5.88	7.00
Perm rods	2.00	2.50
Perm papers	0.53	–
Perm lotion	2.35	2.00
Cotton wool	3.82	7.00
Tint	2.64	4.99
Peroxide 1 l.	0.24	–
Tint brush	1.18	1.00
Tint bowl	1.47	1.50
Bleach	1.18	5.19
Setting mousse	0.94	1.65
Gloves	1.87	1.80
Water spray	3.52	3.00
Appointment book	7.64	5.00
Clippers	35.25	23.00
Highlight cap	7.05	6.00
Sponge	0.35	1.00
TOTAL	163.70	162.78

is a space, one at the back. The sign at the back of a car is probably the most effective because it can be seen most clearly by following vehicles. The signs on the sides will be most visible to clients and their neighbours when you are visiting and your car is parked outside their houses.

There are two types of signs that can be fixed to your car –

magnetic and vinyl. Magnetic signs are usually rectangular or square and have the advantage of being removable, which is very useful when you want to sell your car. These signs will not fall off if they are cared for properly, i.e. removed at least every two weeks and the surface of the car and sign cleaned, removing any dirt and condensation. The cost of three magnetic signs using two or three colours and the name and telephone number of your business will cost around £70.

Vinyl lettering can also be used and is stuck straight on to the car; it costs slightly less than a small magnetic sign but cannot easily be removed. If you plan to use a small van for your business, then to apply a large advertising design will cost around £300.

Calculating potential takings

Here is part of a sample price list (see also Appendix 3), from which you can calculate gross takings over a period of a year using the most popular hairdressing services, usually cutting, blow-drying and perming.

	£
Wet cut	5.00
Blow-dry	5.00
Conditioning Perm	30.00

Assuming your clients are mostly families consisting of a mother who has a perm plus a cut and blow-dry every three months, and a father and two children who have two haircuts each, you could build up your clientele to approximately thirty families if you worked twenty hours per week part-time, or sixty families if you worked forty hours per week full-time. This takes into account one hour travelling time for each family.

Using the sample price list, from each family you could take a *minimum* of £70 every three months. Your annual gross income part-time would be £8,400 and full-time £16,800. To work out the actual profit made, you would then have to deduct all the costs incurred. If you are travelling to the client's house on foot or by bike, there is no cost; however, by car it would vary depending on how far you would have to travel and the amount of petrol used. Therefore, assuming £20 is the cost of a perm and £1 for petrol, deduct these amounts from your total and you will be left with the following:

	£		£
On foot, part-time	8,160	full-time	16,360
By car, part-time	8,400	full-time	16,800

Your National Insurance, liability insurance and any repayment on a car or bike will also have to be deducted, but you would perhaps have to meet such expenses anyway without being in business – and this way the costs are offset against tax. In other words, you pay less tax. This is a very simple example and compares favourably to salon earnings.

On the assumption that your bank manager agrees to grant you an overdraft, you should ascertain the rate of interest, repayments terms, etc. It is only too easy to be delighted that you have obtained financial backing and then to overlook the fact that interest rates, charges, etc. vary considerably. For example, one bank may seek interest at 10% above base rate (currently 6.75%) whereas another will agree to 4%. Then there is the question of bank charges (commission) for, although private banking is effectively free, a business can expect to pay for every conceivable service – such as sending out bank statements, fees for granting an overdraft, fees for renewing an overdraft limit, etc. Also monies paid in (even cash!) will not be cleared (i.e. cannot be drawn upon) for at least three and a half days.

Insurance

The first insurance you must have is called Public Liability Insurance, which covers any claims from your clients. Typically this is £1 million. Depending on the amount of cover you require, it can cost £55–110 per year.

You can also take out an accident policy, which will cover you if you have time off work through sickness or accident. However, the period you have to wait before you get any money is four weeks and the maximum extent of the claim is likely to be two years. Once you have made a claim, the insurance company can refuse cover in subsequent years.

Permanent health insurance can also be taken out. If your gross earnings are £10,000 per year and you are self-employed, this costs approximately £27 per month, increasing yearly by 3, 5 or 7%. Under this sort of policy, you could receive some £86 per week in the event of being unable to work again. If you are signed off work permanently, the government will also pay you currently just under £3,000 per year (approximately £60 per week) depending on your National Insurance contributions.

When buying insurance it is worth shopping around for the best deal and ensuring you buy the right amount of insurance cover. An independent insurance broker can be very helpful.

Professional advice

Business advice can be obtained from your local Business Link or equivalent. In addition, Citizens' Advice Bureaux can advise on any issue and will provide a list of local solicitors who offer fixed fee interviews, costing £10–20 for a half-hour session.

It is probably advisable to employ an accountant, who should be helpful in establishing your tax status as a self-employed person and ensuring *inter alia* that you obtain the appropriate allowances against tax for wear and tear on your car and equipment. You will also need to include in your business expenditure such items as business use of car, electricity, telephone, etc. As anyone can set up in business as an accountant, you would be best to employ a chartered or other qualified accountant. Whilst city accountants may well charge £200 per hour, the small local firm will be more appropriate. You should expect to pay about £100 for the completion of your tax return and any related correspondence. Some accountants will adhere to a fixed hourly rate but others are more flexible and take into account the size of your business. You should try and obtain a fixed quotation for specific services.

4 Personal and Business Management

Getting organized at home

You will need a base from which to run your business and a safe place to store all your equipment and stock (see below). Your home is the obvious place. It is useful to organize yourself before you start with a work station where you have access to telephone, a computer if you have one, a desk for writing and a drawer and shelving where you can store all your related business records and receipts in files. It is important that you do not lose them or let them get damaged. A filing cabinet would be ideal to keep everything altogether. Your stock should be stored, preferably in a metal, lockable cupboard, to keep out children and those who do not understand how to use potentially dangerous products.

The reception of your clients is extremely important since this is potentially the first contact you have with them. Your telephone is in effect your reception so make the most of this tool by practising an excellent telephone manner. If there are other people who have access to your telephone, for example your family, train them to answer it in an appropriate manner during 'business hours', whatever you choose them to be.

You sound better if you stand up and smile when you answer the telephone. It makes your voice sound friendly

41

and clear to your caller. Always have your appointment book and a pen that works to hand; if you fail to do this, you sound very unprofessional when you have to waste your clients' time asking them to wait while you find what you need. Try to predict what clients may ask you and be ready with an informative answer. It is likely that you will be asked what your prices are, so have a current price list pinned to the wall. Alternatively, you may be asked what your hairdressing and beauty qualifications are; give precise details and let the potential client know how many years' experience you have.

There are three different types of telephone to choose from: the basic telephone, an answering machine and a mobile telephone. All three have advantages and dis-advantages.

The basic telephone is the cheapest option because clients telephone you. It can work especially well if you specify a time for clients to phone when you know you are going to be at home, for example between six and eight o'clock in the evening. The disadvantage of this system is that sometimes you may not be able to get home in time for your calls and your clients will then feel frustrated and let down. Once you have regular clients, you can book appointments in advance when you see them; this saves you time and your clients the disappointment of phoning only to find you cannot fit them in. However, a basic telephone is not very flexible because clients cannot reach you easily, especially if they need to cancel their appointments at short notice.

Answering machines are a popular method of ensuring a message does get through to you, but some clients do not like using them, preferring the personal touch, and you may lose potential customers this way. Another disadvantage is that you have to return calls, which costs you money and can be time-consuming, especially when you do not feel up to it at the end of a long, busy day.

A mobile telephone is the most flexible option. If you are travelling over a wide area, it really is essential for the professional freelance hairdresser. By answering the telephone instantly, you are reinforcing the personal nature of your service; clients get instant attention, which is their general expectation today. If you really are too busy with a client or you have switched your phone off to do a quiet massage, there is an answering service available so you can return calls to clients.

Problems with a mobile phone include high rental charges, fraud and poor coverage. As a general rule, the higher the rental the lower the cost of each call, but if you take incoming calls only you will save money. There are two technologies to choose from: analogue and digital. Both use radio signals to transmit calls, but digital signals are computer-coded for better security. Fraud can occur with an analogue phone as it is possible for people to eavesdrop on your calls or to clone your phone and make calls at your expense. Also, there have been reports of some phones being incapable of picking up a strong enough signal in certain areas. Before purchasing, do not sign a contract unless you can test out the phone during a trial period. These contracts are legally binding and, if you decide you no longer want a mobile or you want to change company, it can cost you hundreds of pounds to disconnect. Ask existing phone users in your area about this and make sure you make an informed decision on which type and make to get before you pay out for a whole year's rental.

According to *Which?* (the independent consumer guide) of August 1995, selecting the phone is only part of the buying decision. It is choosing the right tariff and checking the contract carefully that matter the most. Having a mobile telephone may improve your image to your clients and look very professional, but the kind of clientele you have would determine whether this is a viable or necessary option.

Managing client data

Once you start to build up a client base, you will need to store information about your customers, such as their name, address and telephone number. In addition, you should keep client records of perms, tints and other processes, which are important to aid your memory and professional decision-making. If possible, make a note of every visit made, what you did and how much you charged. Use this information to help you identify problem areas, such as poor sales, and then try and improve the situation. It is important to monitor exactly what you are doing all the time.

There are three different ways of storing data. The simplest is to use a book, similar to an address and telephone book, with the alphabet down the side. This method is ideal if you work part-time and do not have too much data. Another method similar to this is a Cardex system, to which you can add more cards under the most popular letters. This method is good because you can carry the cards with you for reference and write them up whilst at the client's house. The index box should stay next to the telephone and you can use it for quick, easy reference, which will sound very professional to any client who phones for information.

If you have a desk computer, it makes sense to use its database. This has the advantage of enabling you to extract the precise information you need; for example, you can target the names and addresses of all your clients in a certain area to promote something at a specific time, ensuring all bookings are close to each other geographically and thus saving you travelling time. Just type in the parameters, and the required data will be available in a moment. A laptop computer would look really professional and you could access information at any time and any place.

As far as the Data Protection Act is concerned, your clients do have the right to see what information is stored about them on your computer but they must write to you first asking permission.

Managing time

Once you start in business it becomes increasingly important to manage your time efficiently. 'Time is money', as the old saying goes, but that does not mean you should work all hours of the day and night to make a living. In order to work effectively, it is worth planning your day to fit in the most important jobs first. An example of priorities, working around clients, could be to start with important ideas when you have maximum energy (your best time may not be first thing in the morning – identify when it actually is), including projects and new work which is thought-provoking or difficult.

The next priority should be tangible, something not too difficult, which shows quicker results and is often apparently urgent. For example, if a client rings up first thing in the morning and you are tempted to fit her in at someone else's expense, through more thorough questioning you may be able to see her at a better time.

Last but not least are the regular and trivial 'housekeeping tasks' requiring little or no thought, such as tidying up your stock cupboard, which can serve as excellent excuses to delay more important tasks.

Practical steps can be taken to improve your time management skills. You can use your diary, not just for appointments and as a reminder of important dates but also to order your day. Begin by making a 'to do action list' each day in your diary. Prioritize the tasks, putting the most important first and ticking each one off as you complete it. You will be amazed at how much you can achieve in a short space of time, and a great deal of satisfaction can be gained from feeling orderly. This will help you to control your use of time rather than letting time control you.

Another aspect of time management is using your time sensibly when deciding how large your area is and how far you are willing to travel to give hairdressing services. It will not necessarily be worth your while to travel ten miles (which could take thirty minutes to an hour depending on where you live) and then to do just one haircut. Your time management and the logistics of getting to clients need to be thought out very carefully and before you start in business you must decide your policy for travel arrangements and the hours you want to work.

Time should be put aside just for thinking and planning. Use slack periods to resolve problems. Think about positive changes in working methods, which could include introducing new or different services, or updating equipment – why not even try designing your own! Think of new ways to promote retail products and increase personal training by acquiring new hairdressing skills or enrolling on a business course.

If you have children of your own to think about when planning your day and you will be taking them with you, then obviously you have other constraints placed upon you. You will need to run a very flexible business because children's needs must come before all else. Most of the time you will be able to juggle business and family very effectively, and if your clients have children too they will be very sympathetic to any cancellations you may have to make at very short notice.

Visiting other homes is good for your children too because meeting new people will boost their confidence. They may have a playmate and different toys to play with; this will make them happy and will help them to be more independent and perhaps less demanding than when they are alone with no one to play with whilst you are trying to work. A supply of drinks and a biscuit seem to work wonders too, if needed. If you have children, it is worth considering buying a car to transport yourselves around as your load will be doubled with hairdressing equipment and children's bits and pieces.

Some clients will request special favours and ask you to fit them into an already busy schedule; you may be tempted to agree because they are good customers. But you must try being more assertive when trying to fit in last-minute appointments. This may sound tricky, but you will work under less pressure if you know you have plenty of time to complete a hairdressing task properly, rather than rushing two clients and losing them both. Always attempt to give an alternative time to your client when it is better for you – and explain why. Never try saving time and taking unnecessary short-cuts because the only thing you will achieve is a dissatisfied clientele. Remember, there are only twenty-four hours in a day and if you intend to keep your clients for a long time, keep their best interests at heart and look after them. It is difficult to be creative when you are tired, so ensure you work sensible hours for both your and the clients' benefit.

Flexibility is the main advantage of working for yourself. You will be able to book yourself 'in' or 'out' depending on your other commitments. After your first year of trading, you will be in a good position to identify the busy and quiet times throughout the year. Obviously, it is better to try and take time off during the quieter times so you do not miss any major business opportunities. Always gives your clients plenty of warning of any plans to be away so that they can be prepared. Do not give your clients the opportunity to go elsewhere.

In conclusion, concentrate on one thing at a time. If you are working on a large project, try to complete little bits at a time; for example, this might include such things as your bookkeeping. Thinking about how you could manage your time more effectively may seem difficult at first but it is worth perservering. If you apply the above steps diligently over a period of time, your improved effectiveness in business will be assured.

Developing negotiating skills

Negotiating skills are needed when you want to agree the way forward with other people, such as your family, peers, clients or business contacts. When negotiating it is important that both parties are satisfied with the outcome, otherwise they will not want to deal with you again. For example, on the personal side, you may want to work an extra evening one week because it will be profitable. However, you know your partner will have objections. How can this situation be handled effectively?

To start with, it is worth knowing in your own mind what

you are willing to concede in another area which your partner finds attractive. You could then make a reasonable proposal such as, 'If you stay in on Tuesday evening, then I will do your ironing on Wednesday'. An agreement may be reached at this point, but on the other hand your proposal may not be attractive enough to your partner, who may suggest another reward. Listen to that proposal and if it is acceptable to you, finish the negotiation by summarizing what has been said and agreed upon.

The negotiations are always open until the other party says 'No'. At this point, you must respect the other person's decision and direct your negotiations elsewhere. Remember to open with a reasonable proposal, listen to what the other person's expectations are and confirm the agreed final decision.

Solving problems

Inevitably, there will be times when you face problems in business that may need much thought. To help you, here is a simple method by which you can look at the problem. It simplifies and clarifies and at the same time should aid you in your problem-solving and decision-making. Once a problem is identified it is usually much easier to solve it.

On one side of plain paper, write down the problem; for example, 'I do not have enough clients'. Turn the paper over and think of about ten other problems related to the first problem over the page. Scatter the problems across the page, avoiding list-making. If you are having difficulty thinking of things, put anything even if it feels irrelevant to start with – and don't worry if you cannot think of ten things. Your list might include the following:

- No one phones me for appointments.
- I can't get to my clients on time.
- I do not have an answering machine.
- My bike keeps getting punctures.
- I do not have enough money to advertise.

- I do not have enough time to promote my business.
- I never seem to have the right equipment or stock in my bag when I need it.
- I keep forgetting stock and equipment.

Now that your problems are scattered across the page, group similar problems together like this:

- No one telephones me.
- I do not have an answering machine.
- Clients complain they can never get hold of me.

- I can't get to my clients on time.
- My bike keeps getting punctures.

- I do not have enough money to advertise.
- I do not have enough time to promote my business.

- I never seen to have the right equipment or stock in my bag when I need it.
- I keep forgetting equipment.

Your page will probably have three or four big groups on it. Look at each group and solve each problem. It is clear from the above that this person lacks organizational and communication skills. However, this method shows that there is a need to prioritize by fixing the bike properly or taking another route which does not cause punctures and by making sure time is allocated through time management to promote the business. As far as the clients are concerned, they could be informed of the best times to phone and the hairdresser could have a prompt list of questions by the telephone to create confidence. In addition, a checklist of equipment could be used so that nothing is forgotten at each visit. This method is a powerful tool which can be applied to any problem. Try it and see.

Mastering Total Quality Management

Total Quality Management is a concept which may not readily be associated with a sole trader but more often with a large company. The idea is certainly one which can be implemented fully to improve general management of your business. It is all about identifying areas of costs to a business in terms of wasted time or wasted resources.

Total Quality Management (or Quality Management generally) is a method of conforming to the requirements that give the client satisfaction in all respects – product or service, due date, delivery and price. The other aspect of this idea is that the clients' requirements can be identified and measured. This may sound confusing, but for a freelance hairdresser it means that everything you do for a client is recorded, and in your case details of information will be on the client record card and in your diary/appointment book. In your appointment book, details of distances travelled are not written down as such but mileage can be calculated because you know the distances and time involved to get to your clients. From this data you can identify better ways of doing things in terms of saving time and money, as a result of which your business will increase its profitability.

In Quality Management the fact that we all have customers to look after is identified. This creates a chain and if the chain is broken, the customer will suffer as a consequence. The hairdressing business chain is as follows: manufacturer; wholesaler/retail outlets; salons/freelance hairdresser; clients. In the light of this, we can expect quality service from the wholesaler as well as providing it to our clients.

There are four classic Quality sayings that are worth repeating: 'Get it right first time', a self-explanatory saying, will be beneficial to your client and will save you time in extra visits and stock if you get it wrong and need to put it right; 'How am I doing?' suggests that you must always assess exactly how well you are performing in terms of client satisfaction, costs to your business and your own personal development within the business; 'How can I make it better?' builds on 'How am I doing?' by ensuring you get your service right first time, by cutting back on any unnecessary costs and by actually doing something for yourself, such as getting yourself more training or improving your own time management skills; 'Say what you do, do what you say you do, record what you do and monitor what you do' is fairly self-explanatory and builds trust between you and your clients. It also ensures that you run a very professional business which is well disciplined and effective, because you know exactly the progress you are making at all times. You will also be aware of any weaknesses which may be apparent, but you can then do something positive to correct the situation.

Quality is aiming for a perfect world and excellence for your clients – this is done first by formulating a Mission Statement, which for a freelance hairdresser could be: 'To provide a high-quality hairdressing service to meet the special needs of each customer, providing me with a satisfying job and high profit.' Next, identify who your customers are and their requirements. Then implement these requirements and check, through client feedback, that they are getting what they want. Ensure the feedback is collated, monitored and then acted upon. Consistent, excellent service is what your clients expect, every time.

Recording your finances

You will need to record all your financial transactions, even if you are taking less than the annual tax threshold which is £3,765 for 1996/7 and £4,045 for 1997/8. If you have given up your previous employment, your employer should give you a P45 which shows your PAYE code, total pay so far in the tax year and the amount of tax paid. This must be sent to your local tax office.

The Inland Revenue requires all self-employed people to request a self-assessment tax return which will be issued on the 6 April. This should be returned to them by 30 September, when the tax office will calculate the amount of tax due for you. Alternatively it should be returned by 31 January if you prefer to calculate your own tax. If the tax return is returned after 31 January deadline, then financial penalties will be incurred. In the past tax was calculated upon trading profits for the twelve-month period ending in the tax year before the year covered by the return. Now, however, if from 1995/6 you have become self-employed, tax is calculated on the profits arising in the tax year itself.*

Keep all records and retain them for seven years. Back-up records, such as invoices, receipts, bank statements and paying-in slips, should also be kept to show where the income came from. Ensure that all business and personal expenses are kept separate. For example, if you use the same vehicle for both business and private purposes, keep a record of business and private mileage and split the vehicle running costs in the appropriate proportions.

Bookkeeping

There are different methods of recording business transactions and you will find various types of account books at stationery shops. Some are for recording each day's takings and all other transactions as they occur; other account books are ruled into columns and you can add headings according to your needs. However, the simplest and cheapest option is to start with a small notebook.

At the front of the book, write down the date and record how much money you have received from clients, including tips. At the back, record exactly how much you have spent on running the business. This will include items such as stock, the cost of your uniform, running costs of vehicles, advertising, telephone charges, normal accountancy fees and the cost of replacing worn-out tools with new ones. Examples of expenses which are only partly allowable are the rent, rates, lighting and heating bills of premises that are

* Please contact the Inland Revenue for further information.

also used for domestic purposes. If you employ a member of your family in your business, for example as a receptionist, their wages are an allowable expense as long as you do in fact pay them.

Keep all your receipts, date and number them as soon as they are received and record them in your notebook (or a daybook, as it is known in accountancy terminology). This makes references back through your accounts much easier. The receipts would be represented by invoices from the wholesaler, cheques you have cashed and any cash receipts from clients which are not banked. This information is then organized for yourself or your accountant to prepare your tax returns. For example, at the front of the book, record your takings *into* the business:

TAKINGS FOR JUNE

	£
21 June	
Perm	25.00
3 × cut and blow-dry	30.00
TOTAL	55.00
22 June	
Tint	20.00
5 × cut and blow-dry	50.00
Perm	30.00
TOTAL	100.00

Continue until you complete a month and then insert a running total like this:

TOTAL TAKINGS	
FOR JUNE	1,600.00

This information records all your takings into the business, whilst the back of the book shows everything you have spent going *out* of the business, such as stock you had to buy, petrol for your car or payment of your telephone bill. Your book will look something like this:

OUTGOINGS FOR JUNE

	£
21 June	
Tint	5.00
(receipt number 21)	
22 June	
Telephone bill	25.00
(receipt number 22)	
25 June	
Petrol	15.00
(receipt number 23)	
30 June	
Drawings	60.00
(receipt number 24)	
TOTAL OUTGOINGS FOR JUNE	105.00

At the end of every twelve months of trading, all businesses have to produce final accounts for the benefit of their owners, the Inland Revenue and the VAT office. This period of twelve months is called the business financial year and it can run from any month of the year, though two months are particularly popular: January, because it is the start of the calendar year, and April, because it is the start of the tax year. The tax year runs from 6 April to the following 5 April. Tax returns can be worked out by yourself or by taking your daybook, receipts and bank statements to an accountant. None the less whoever prepares your accounts, you are still responsible, as the business owner, for their accuracy and for correctly declaring the amounts of profits. Even if you plan to employ an accountant, it is still worth having some accountancy knowledge so that you understand some of the terms used.

If you think you will be taking more than £15,000 gross per annum and are considering doing all your own bookkeeping, it would be advisable to take a practical bookkeeping course, details of which can be found at your local further education or adult education college. Key accounting terms include:

Assets – things of monetary value owned by a person or business, such as money, equipment, stock and transport.

Capital – the value of assets held by the owner of the business.

Liabilities – an amount of money which is owed, for example a mortgage. The relationship between assets and ownership is shown by a simple statement known as the accounting equation:

Assets = Capital + Liabilities

The accounting equation can be used to work out any one of the parts as long as the details of the other two are known. If the value of assets and liabilities is known, the capital can be worked out like this:

Assets − Liabilities = Capital

Balance sheet – an itemized list of assets, capital and liabilities of a business. It applies on the date when the balance sheet is drawn up, which is usually the last day of a trading period.

Ledger – the term used to describe books of account.

Account – a historical record of monetary movements in chronological order.

Credits and debits – a credit is when money is put into an account and a debit is an expense which results in a decrease in an asset or an increase in a liability. As can be seen from the accounting equation, this means that the capital is reduced by each expense. Debits and credits of accounts are recorded in a ledger, as shown below:

ACCOUNT TITLE

Debit side	Credit side

Profit – the difference between total income (revenue earned) and the total expenses incurred during the same period of time.

Gross profit – the excess of sales over the cost of goods sold.

Net profit – what remains after all other costs have been deducted from the gross profit.

Profit and loss account – part of a business's final accounts, showing the profit or loss a business has made.

Double-entry bookkeeping – a method whereby two entries are made in the accounts for every transaction: debit one account and credit another.

Depreciation – the measure of the estimated loss in monetary value of a fixed asset owing to use; it reduces profit because it increases cost to the business. Yearly depreciation can be worked out by dividing the expected cost by the expected lifespan, but it depends on certain unpredictables such as damage.

Accounts which the tax office may ask for are usually in two parts: the profit and loss account and the balance sheet. The profit and loss account shows whether a business has made a profit or a loss and is a summary of the year's trading transactions. Apart from tax purposes, this will also help when comparing planned profit against actual profit and when making adjustments in business strategy in order to plan ahead. The balance sheet shows the assets and the liabilities of the business at a moment in time, with the former shown on the left-hand side and the latter on the right-hand side. For an example of a profit and loss account and a balance sheet, see Appendix 1a.

Another way to record your transactions is on your computer; this is done with a spreadsheet package, of which there are a few on the market. An example of a spreadsheet can be found in Appendix 1. The advantages of using a computer are that you do not have to add up any sums yourself, and if you are planning to sell hairdressing products it will save you time when faced with long lists of stock. Another advantage of using the computer is that you can ask 'what if' questions. This means, for example, that if you want to know how much you would have to take to make £100 extra profit in a month, it is a matter of pressing a couple of keys and the answer will appear, instead of doing long calculations by hand. It would be worth doing an information technology course that includes spreadsheets and word processing (if you have not already done so) to help you get started.

For tax purposes, if you choose to keep your records on a computer do not forget to keep the original paper record of your sales, purchases and similar transactions, unless you have access to an optical imaging system or can microfilm all your original documents.

Hairdressing equipment and stock checklist

Every time you visit clients, you must protect them and their homes from damage. Therefore, these items are essential for every visit:

- Protection for the floor – washable sheeting is available for this purpose.
- Protection for the chairs – plastic covers are available from your hairdressing supplies wholesaler.
- Gowns and towels for the client.

Protect your clients from cross-infection by ensuring that equipment is always kept clean. Scrub combs and brushes between clients, using hot soapy water, and wipe scissor blades regularly with disinfectant. Your hands should always be washed before each client and do not eat or smoke whilst working.

Always dispose of waste carefully, especially such items as used razors. If possible, a first-aid kit should be available for use. If you have to walk to clients' homes, this may not be practical but if you have a car, then keep one in there. First-aid kits are available from most chemists.

Here is a general checklist to serve as a reminder of items

you will need to take with you for each process:

Cut and blow-dry
Gown for client and overall/apron for yourself
Two coloured towels
Small bottles of shampoo and conditioner
Scissors and clippers with attachments
Combs, brushes and neck brush
Hairdryer and/or diffuser
Tongs
Hairspray and setting aid

Cut, shampoo and set
Gown for client and overall/apron for yourself
Two coloured towels
Shampoo and conditioner
Scissors
Combs, brushes and neck brush
Hairdryer
Hairspray and setting aid
Rollers, pins and hairnet

Perming
Two gowns for client and overall/apron for yourself
Five white towels and two spare coloured towels
Shampoo and conditioner
Rubber/plastic gloves
Perm lotion and neutralizer
Perm curlers
Plastic protective strips
Cotton wool strips and end papers
Plastic cap
Combs, brushes and neck brush
Hairdryer and/or diffuser
Tongs
Hairspray and setting aid
If setting afterwards, rollers, pins and hairnet

Tinting
Gown and protective cape for client and overall/apron for yourself
Three black towels
Shampoo and conditioner
Rubber/plastic gloves
Tint brush and bowl
Tint and peroxide
Cotton wool
Plastic cap
Tin foil
Combs (including wide-toothed) and brushes
Hairdryer
Tongs
Hairspray and setting aid
If setting afterwards, rollers, pins and hairnet

Highlighting or bleaching
Gown and protective cape for client and overall/apron for yourself
Two white towels and two spare coloured towels
Shampoo and conditioner
Rubber/plastic gloves
Tint brush and bowl
Bleach, toner and peroxide
Highlight cap and hook
Cotton wool
Plastic cap
Tin foil
Combs and brushes
Hairdryer
Tongs
Hairspray and setting aid

Hair extensions
Gown for client and overall/apron for yourself
Two coloured towels
Shampoo and conditioner

Scissors
Hair extensions kit
Combs and brushes
Hairdryer
Tongs
Hairspray and setting aid

Other essentials
Street map
Spare hose for taps or a large plastic jug
Water spray
Back mirror

Stock and equipment tips

- Keep stock and equipment costs down by choosing good-quality brands that won't let you down and hair preparations that work effectively and give excellent results every time.
- Cut down on waste by choosing perm solution you can dispense yourself and thus take only as much as you need.
- Save space and money by buying 18% peroxide and dilute it to the strength desired. Remember to keep all chemicals such as peroxide and perm lotion locked up, away from children. Ensure you use a precise measuring beaker with a lip for easy pouring and mix the correct amounts required.

Stock purchase

Stock can be bought either from wholesalers or direct from the manufacturer. Use the Yellow Pages for details. You will have more choice of products if you visit the wholesalers and there is the added advantage of convenience; as a busy hairdresser you will save time (which costs money) rather than shopping around to save what could be quite small amounts. If you have only one account to settle each month, this also saves time and record-keeping – and thus money.

Laundry

When doing the laundry for your business, using your own washing machine and tumble dryer is the most economical and convenient way to wash and dry your towels and gowns. If this is not possible, then the launderette is the only other option open to you. Unfortunately, constant trips will create extra costs in terms of time and laundry charges. All towels, gowns and overalls should be washed after use. Do not risk reusing soiled laundry as your clients will notice and not return.

Make your towels last much longer and avoid scruffy, splodgy, unsightly specimens by using the correct colour of towel for the right job. Use coloured towels for shampooing and cutting, black for all your colouring jobs (from coloured setting aids to tinting) and white for bleaching.

Getting to your client's house

Walking is the cheapest option but is time-consuming. However, if you live in or near a block of flats or in a small area where you have lots of clients who live close to each other, this will be a very convenient way to travel.

Carry your equipment in a shopping trolley or in a rucksack, both of which can be personalized in some way. A rucksack will be a very practical option if you are going up and down stairs.

Travelling by pedal bike or motorbike is another inexpensive option compared to a car. Use a basket and a top box as well as a rucksack to carry your equipment.

A car or van is probably the most convenient mode of transport, especially if you have to travel long distances. It is also the most expensive to buy and run. However, as with a bike, any expenses can be offset against tax.

5 Health and Safety Aspects at Work and at Home

It is the duty of every freelance hairdresser, as far as is reasonably practicable, to ensure the safety of their clients whilst in their homes. It is also important when self-employed to avoid having unplanned time off work due to illness or as the result of an accident. Here is some quick, basic practical advice to protect you and your client:

- Do not let flexes trail across the floor, which could cause someone to trip.
- Never touch electrical switches and electrical appliances with wet hands.
- Keep floors dry and free of spills.
- Ventilate the room by opening a window if you are using chemicals.
- Carry a first-aid box with you.

Health and safety regulations

New health and safety regulations came into force on 1 January 1990. (A guide is available from the Health and Safety regulator – the local number can be found in the telephone directory.) These are generally referred to as COSHH, which stands for 'Control of Substances Hazardous to Health', and apply to substances with the following classifications:

- Very toxic
- Toxic
- Harmful
- Corrosive
- Irritant

All of these descriptions can be applied to hairdressing products. To find out the precise effects of chemicals, a data sheet can be obtained from different manufacturers to enable proper risk assessment. This information must be taken into consideration when starting up and running your business. Here is a list of products and their dangers, and precautions which should be taken to ensure the safety of you and your client.

PRODUCT	DANGERS	PRECAUTIONS
Chemicals		
Perms, neutralizer, tint, bleach, peroxide, hairspray and setting aids	Fire, poisoning, spillage, chemical burns, explosion	Refer to the respective regulations before handling. Clearly label all bottles and jars. Store aerosols in a cool place. Store inflammables, such as setting aids, and perm lotion, in a shed, garage or fireproof cabinet away from your home. A prominent sign must be displayed on the front of all chemical storage areas, e.g. DANGER – POISONOUS AND INFLAMMABLE CHEMICALS. KEEP AWAY FROM CHILDREN. NO SMOKING ALLOWED. Store large containers low down to reduce risks when handling.

Gowns and protective coverings	Insufficient protection against allergies	Protect yourself from spillage of any harmful liquids. Avoid sandals and choose flat, non-slip shoes. Wear rubber gloves when handling any hairdressing chemicals.

Electrical and mechanical

Clippers	Electric shock, small cuts and nicks, pulling hair out of scalp	Hold clippers at correct angle, flex out of the way. Keep the blades clean, sharp and oiled. *Do not use electric clippers on wet hair*.
Tongs, crimping irons and heated rollers	Burns and electric shock	Keep away from skin and scalp – holding them on the hair burns and damages it.
Ear piercing	Fainting, minor shock, post-treatment infection	Ensure client is seated and hair is clean and away from the ears. Bathe ear lobe with surgical spirit. Do not repierce over scar tissue. Give after-care instructions.
Electrical equipment	Electric shock, burns, falls due to trailing flexes and fires due to electrical faults	Ensure that all electrical appliances are correctly fused and earthed. Arrange for an electrician to check all your equipment every six months and carry out any repairs. In between, check the flex

yourself for any splits and
replace if necessary.
Do not leave flexes trailing
across the floor.
Keep water away from electrical equipment and sockets.
Do not overload adaptors

Cleaning of equipment

When travelling to clients, it is not practical to carry
sterilization equipment such as an autoclave with you, and
so other effective methods have to be found to keep brushes,
combs and scissors clean for individual clients, thus avoiding
cross-infection. The application of heat is the simplest and
most effective method. Wash equipment through with hot
soapy water between each client and wipe the blades of
scissors with disinfectant.

Basic first-aid

If you are suddenly faced with an emergency, try not panic
because you need to be able to think clearly and be
supportive towards the victim. Dial 999 or go straight to
hospital if a person becomes unconscious, has serious burns,
you suspect poisoning, you cannot stop bleeding, the person
has difficulty breathing, there is severe pain or there is
bleeding from an ear.

When you are working be especially vigilant when
children are around; they do not understand potential
dangers. Warn them if they come too close to tongs or want
to touch equipment and lotions. Here is a list of first-aid
techniques which may be useful:

Head injuries

- Gently move person into the recovery position with
  head to one side so the tongue cannot fall back and
  prevent breathing.

65

- If broken bones are suspected, do not move limbs.

Burns and scalds

- Reduce heat of a very small burn or scald by holding the burnt area under a cold-water tap for at least ten minutes. If clothing has become burnt or charred it must be expertly removed.
- Cover burn with a clean, smooth cloth or cling film to avoid infection.

Poisoning

- Ensure the patient drinks as much water or milk as possible to dilute the poison but don't make the person sick because some substances do more damage coming up than going down.
- Keep a sample of the substance to show to the doctor and get medical advice as soon as possible.

Bleeding

- Clean with water – not antiseptic.
- Stop the bleeding by applying pressure to the cut, preferably with a pad of clean cloth or your hand.
- Get medical help if the wound is dirty or there is something stuck in it.

Choking

- If a child, hold upside down or (if too large) hold the head well down over your knee or a chair.
- Slap between shoulder blades up to four times and remove the object only if it can be done easily.

The first-aid box

If you are travelling to clients on foot or on your bicycle, it will be difficult to carry much more than essentials in your bag. You will definitely need such items as waterproof plasters in case you accidentally cut yourself. You must also keep important information about yourself recorded in your diary, in case you have an accident either on the way to/from work or at work. If you use a car or van to travel to clients, it is advisable to keep an up-to-date, comprehensive first-aid box (identified by a white cross on a green background) in your vehicle at all times. Essential items include:

- Emergency information card – containing such information as telephone numbers (e.g. local hospital), contact numbers for family, next-of-kin blood groups, religion and allergies of family members.
- Special personal medication – such as spare asthma inhaler.
- Notebook and pencil – to keep a record of any client accidents and the treatment given. This is to avert any subsequent problem, e.g. allergic reaction to plaster.
- Individually wrapped plasters of assorted sizes – these should include some waterproof plasters, effective when washing and handling wet hair.
- Pack of multi-purpose wet wipes
- Individually wrapped sterile dressings of assorted sizes
- Non-allergic adhesive tape roll
- Eye pads with bandage attachment
- Triangular bandages (minimum two)
- Crêpe bandage
- Safety pins
- Roll of cotton wool
- Scissors
- Tweezers
- Disposable gloves
- Plastic bag for rubbish
- Insect bite medication
- Unbreakable thermometer

Looking after yourself

You should give due care and attention not only to your clients but also to yourself. When self-employed, it is easy to skip the essentials – such as meals. Give yourself enough time to eat properly and avoid eating food that has a high fat, salt or sugar content. Exercisely regularly and have enough sleep to recharge yourself for your next business challenge.

Coping with stress

Stress is something we all experienced to a lesser or greater degree at some point in our lives, but it has a positive as well as a negative side to it.

On the negative side, stress levels increase when we find ourselves in disagreeable situations, like overworking or getting held up in a traffic jam. As a result, some people may experience physical effects, such as headaches, high blood-pressure, ulcers, insomnia or some forms of arthritis and asthma. Alternatively, on the positive side, life without stress and the energy it gives would be unbearably dull and nothing would ever be achieved. Stress motivates us to earn a living and give our best performance.

An awareness of the need to balance stress levels, and the ability to handle them by developing a set of stress skills that are right for you as an individual, will enable you to learn to make positive decisions and choices. When faced with a set of circumstances, for example ill health or a packed appointments book, you need to respond in a physical and psychological way. The way in which you react to stressful situations should be channelled correctly so as to keep stress levels down. Stress is not the same as pressure, although pressure can contribute to the creation of stress. A pressured situation can be rewarding, provided you can see your way out of it.

Working for yourself offers genuine job satisfaction and a feeling of being in control of your own destiny. However, it can be an isolating business, and feelings of isolation can be notoriously stressful. There is always the temptation to overwork and if you are a sole trader you will have no one to whom you can delegate. However, steps can be taken to help yourself, as follows:

- Be strict about your hours of business and keep your home and work lives as separate as possible.
- Manage your time effectively and plan ahead to avoid rushing and resultant stressful situations.
- Take out health insurance if you are worried about taking time away from the business due to illness.
- Employ a recommended accountant if you are worried about any financial aspects.
- Think positively in all situations, see problems as potential opportunities.
- Learn to value physical fitness as a means of relaxation and an antidote to stress, and do all you can to acquire it.

Finally, research has shown that if people meet regularly in a group to exchange funny experiences, the act of laughing can make the muscles relax and stress diminish. As a freelance hairdresser there are lots of opportunities to do this, so go and enjoy yourself!

Protecting yourself

Your personal safety is a factor to consider when you advertise publicly and when you are travelling on your own. Most of the time you will be safe, but you never know who might be inviting you into their home or who is helping you with your car or bike if you break down. Take precautions to protect yourself – these could include travelling with a companion and having a mobile telephone. If you are out and about and you break down, always telephone for help; do not try to flag someone down. Always let others know where you are going to be and at what times, especially with new clients you do not know. If possible, ask a friend to accompany you on a first visit to any client who has made you feel uneasy.

Prevention is better than cure, so make sure you do not put yourself in danger by visiting a place or area where you know there is a high risk of trouble. If possible, learn how to fix simple problems on your bike or car. The RAC has started running women's workshops in response to requests from its female members and Peugeot has also introduced Women at the Wheel workshops, offering instruction in maintenance, wheel changing and repair charge estimates.

Bike repairs

One of the most common problems with push-bikes is having a puncture. If you can be totally self-sufficient and do not need to seek help when fixing it, you will be safer and will get to your destination faster. The task of fixing a puncture takes only ten minutes – with practice. You will need the basic bike kit, which includes three tyre levers, a puncture repair kit, a universal spanner and a pump.

Method
1. Let the air out of the tyre (if there is any left) by taking the tyre valve off (it may be a screw type).
2. Prise one edge of the tyre off the rim with tyre levers, by inserting two levers approximately 15 cm apart.
3. Work the third lever or your fingers around the edge of the tyre, taking it off the rim all the way round.
4. Push the valve part of the inner tube through the rim and remove the inner tube from the tyre.
5. Put the valve back on to the inner tube.
6. Blow up the inner tube.
7. Listen for air escaping (a 'sssss' sound!).
8. Take the crayon out of the puncture repair kit and draw a circle around the puncture.
9. Let the air out of the inner tube again.
10. Put some glue over the puncture, ensuring that the area

covered is larger than the patch chosen.

11. Take the backing off the patch.
12. When the glue is slightly tacky, affix the patch, smoothing down and making sure there are no gaps.
13. Take the other backing off the patch.
14. Rub the chalk on the grater found on the puncture repair box and sprinkle it over the repair so that it gets a light dusting.
15. Put the valve back on and pump up the inner tube, checking to see there are no other punctures.
16. Put the valve back in the hole in the wheel rim and push the inner tube back inside the tyre.
17. Using your fingers, pinch back the tyre all around the rim – you may need a tyre lever for the last section.
18. Pump a few times and then check around the tyre to ensure that the inner tube has not been 'pinched'.
19. Pump tyre up fully.
20. Off you go!

Car trouble

Cars are just as liable to suffer from punctures as bikes and it is just as important to be familiar with vehicle tyre-changing techniques. It is never pleasant to be stranded on the roadside with this problem, but practice makes perfect and your familiarity with this process will reduce the stress of having to deal with it when it occurs. The task should take approximately twenty minutes to complete.

Method

1. Pull over as soon as you feel you have a flat tyre, as quickly as is safe – it feels like you are driving in sand.
2. Put your emergency warning lights on and turn the rest of your lights off.
3. Ensure you are in a safe place and change the tyre. If not, *leave the car* and the area. If necessary, ask the police for assistance and they will help. If it is safe but your car is on a steep slope, you must ask for help to get

71

the car on to level ground.

4. Open the boot of your car and find the spare tyre, which is usually under the matting of the boot. Attached to or underneath the spare tyre, there will be a wheel brace (a big spanner) and a jack, the device which lifts up the car. Wheel-brace extensions can be purchased for better leverage. Take them out of the car.

5. Go to the side of the car where the puncture is. Look under the car between the wheels, close to the puncture wheel. You are looking for a jack point – where the jack slots in.

6. Put the jack under the jack point and wind it up until it fits into the slot, finger tight. *Do not start lifting the car at this point. Check that the handbrake is on.*

7. Take off the hub-caps and loosen the wheel nuts with the wheel brace. This may take a bit of effort, and if you cannot manage it you may have to ask someone to help.

8. Wind up the jack until the car is *just* clear of the ground.

9. Undo and take off the wheel nuts.

10. Lift the wheel off its stud and lay it flat on the ground – otherwise it may roll away.

11. Put on the spare wheel.

12. Do up the wheel nuts alternately to ensure that the wheel is attached evenly. Make sure that the wheel nuts are tight.

13. Lower the jack.

14. Try the nuts again to make sure they are tight. (If you are not sure, drive to the nearest garage and ask a mechanic to check them.)

15. Replace the hub-caps.

16. Put the punctured wheel, jack and brace in the boot.

17. Take the punctured tyre to the garage to be fixed and replace in the boot.

Every day you must check you have enough petrol so you are not caught short, and once a week it is advisable to check the oil, tyre pressures and water for your windscreen. You should also wash your car weekly to keep it clean and smart.

6   Caring for Clients

Your clients are the most important part of your business; without them you have no business, so their needs and expectations must be met. Excellent communication skills are essential to ensure that you continually assess clients' needs and provide levels of service beyond what they expect or have become used to expecting; such skills start with your telephone manner (see Chapter 4) and move right through to handling complaints. You will be in competition with others who are offering a similar service, and so to keep your clients you must continuously provide them with a high-quality service.

Your work should always be of the highest standard. It is always worth spending enough time on whatever you are doing and getting it absolutely right before moving on to the next stage. Check and double check haircuts, perms, tints, etc. Ensure that timings of processes are accurate; one or two minutes over the process time for a perm can make the difference between a firm wave and frizz.

As a freelance hairdresser you should be able to create all the styles that your clients will ever want. Keep up-to-date with new trends and styles by reading the national trade magazines and being aware of local, popular preferences. When new techniques and products come on to the market it is always worth trying them out, especially if your clients show an interest in them. Always try and be one step ahead of your competition and offer products that are not generally available.

Research has shown that in most cases clients put the following factors in this order of importance:

1. Availability of your service or products
2. Friendly and quality service
3. Punctuality
4. Pricing
5. New products
6. Advertising

Whatever the above list suggests, however, all of your clients are individuals and they may possibly rank each factor differently. It is up to you to find out what each of your clients wants from you.

Initial consultation

The best time to establish a client's needs is at the initial consultation; here you must find out as much as possible about your customers and their lifestyles. This will influence the options of suitable hair-styles and hair colour available to them. The initial consultation should be arranged before or at the beginning of the first appointment. It should be a two-way process, with your client doing most of the talking. This advice is usually offered free of charge, especially since it is in your interest to get the information right first time.

The kinds of questions you could ask might include what type of job or hobbies they have, how much time they want to spend on their hair and how proficient they are at styling it. For example, if a client enjoys swimming regularly, an easy-care style will be ideal.

Involve your clients by asking their opinion and listening to any ideas they have had. Clients have usually thought long and hard about their hair and usually have their own idea about the direction they want to take. Suggest options available to them that they may not have considered: cut, colour, perm – there is so much to choose from. Then, if they need help, make it easier for them to decide and say which way you think would look best. This will either confirm what they were thinking all along or give them something to think about for another time. Whatever your conclusions, be confident; your clients will want to feel that you know what you are doing and are capable of coming up with 'the new me'.

Meeting new clients is rather like starting a journey together, with both of you knowing how to get from 'here' to 'there' through discussion of your shared objectives and thoughts on how they might change in the future.

Clients' needs

In addition to having their hair styled, your clients will come to you for other reasons too. These will include the following:

- Relaxation
- Morale boosting
- Value for money
- Companionship

Clients who just want to relax are unlikely to want to talk about the things they normally do. They are probably very busy people who are communicating all the time and who may not want to start talking or listening again (perhaps this is how you feel after a long day at work). Instead, such clients may prefer very little or no conversation and perhaps a few well-chosen magazines which they might find interesting. All they are likely to want is to be pampered without having to make any decisions. It is then completely appropriate that you take the initiative, checking occasionally that you are providing the right level of service.

For those clients who feel a bit low and have perhaps suffered something stressful that has affected their lives, a boost and a change of image may be their priority; in this context livelier conversation is more appropriate, in contrast to the client who wishes to relax. Be enthusiastic and experiment using the hair-storming method (see Chapter 7) of finding the best style for your client.

Getting value for money is everyone's concern, but this is especially so for those whose finances are limited, perhaps because they are unemployed, disabled or on a low income, or because they are on a student grant or at home with a family. Cost is important to them but a high-quality hairstyle is still the top priority.

Those clients who want companionship whilst they are having their hair styled will probably just want to talk. These clients may have little contact with other people and may therefore enjoy telling you about their past, their family, their dog, their problems – anything. All you should do is listen and catch the best time during a pause to ask, 'How much hair would you like trimmed off today?' It is almost as if they need to unload thousands of words in the time you are with them.

Another type of client – likely to be from either the 'value-for-money' or the 'companionship' group – is the one who loves to complain. Such hard-to-please clients are in fact most precious to hairdressers (or anyone in business) because they tell you exactly what they think about the last perm, colour, cut or whatever, with no holds barred. This is the best feedback you will probably ever receive, so listen very carefully and take mental notes of how you can improve your service. Other clients may not complain like this, but they may think the same things and won't ask you to come back again if they are dissatisfied in any way. Just think what a challenge this is and how wonderful it will be the next time you return to such clients and they don't complain!

You are aiming to provide a good service for all types of people who all have different needs. If you are always ready to smile and be sympathetic before you have even touched their hair, you will be halfway towards building a successful business relationship.

Clients with disabilities

It is likely that you will meet clients who have disabilities, with their own special needs. The Disability Etiquette leaflet published by The Employers' Forum on Disability offers helpful advice. The excerpt given below indicates the general common courtesies that should be observed:

- Offer assistance to a disabled person if you feel like it, but wait until your offer is accepted before you help. Do not assume you know the best way of helping.
- Listen to any instruction you are given. Treat adults in a manner befitting adults. For example, only call a person by their first name when extending that familiarity to others present.
- Do not use gestures more suitable for children, such as patting a wheelchair user on the head. Do not lean on a person's wheelchair. The chair is part of the body space of the person who uses it. Make appropriate physical contact with disabled people according to the situation, as you would anyone else. For example, give a handshake or put an arm round the shoulders. Talk directly to a disabled person rather than through a companion. Relax and make eye contact.
- Do not be embarrassed about using common expressions, such as 'See you later' or 'I'll be running along then', which may relate to the person's impairment.
- When planning an event, ask advice from disabled people and advertise accessibility. If access and facilities are not clearly described, disabled people may not risk coming because of previous difficulties.
- Do not make assumptions about the existence or absence of disabilities. Some people have hidden disabilities, such as diabetes or mental health problems.

Client loyalty

Complete client loyalty is what all hairdressers are aiming for. In addition to the methods given above, there are several further ways of building it up. You may wish to consider the following:

- Giving special concessions to long-standing clients, for example a free haircut after every £100 spent with you.
- Selling gift vouchers.
- Sending greetings cards on special occasions that your client may have mentioned and that you have put in your diary.
- Cutting out any articles from magazines or papers that you think may be of interest to your clients.

Establishing a complaints and guarantees procedure

When offering your service, make your complaints and guarantees procedure clear. Here is an example of a policy you can use:

- Make it easy for clients to express their wishes by creating a friendly and open environment.
- If a client is dissatisfied with a colour or perm, you must be informed as soon as possible (and within the maximum period of a week from the initial appointment) so you can put it right.
- Let the client know exactly how long she can reasonably expect her perm or colour to last before you do it again, so that she has realistic expectations.
- Any product which your client is dissatisfied with will be replaced immediately.

To avoid having to deal with any clients' complaints, make sure you are *on time*; if you are going to be early or late, ring and ask them if it is still convenient. Give all your clients the special attention they deserve and help them to buy your services and products. A positive and sincere attitude towards your customers is essential: so too are consistency and reliability. Always say what you are going to do – and do it right first time and on time.

Developing client services

Individuals and families

Individuals and families will usually have their hair styled at home. Families are more cost-effective for your business because you can usually do more than one client's hair during a single visit. The hours you work will probably be fairly social because children are not likely to have their hair cut late at night or too early in the morning; however, you may want to consider working at weekends since this is when most families are at home.

Children

Children are potentially your most important first clients. Quite often you may find that mothers will have their children's hair cut first; if they think you are good enough, they will then have their hair done! You could help to make children's first haircuts a more pleasurable experience by providing the following:

- A choice of children's videos
- Colourful 'Well Done' stick-on badges or, if parents agree, a sweet
- A bright gown that is practical and fun to wear
- A first haircut envelope or a certificate on which a small cutting of the hair is attached.

Weddings

Wedding work is usually carried out in homes. Your services will be required on the 'big day', and in addition it is customary for the bride-to-be to have a practice session beforehand to ensure the perfect style is achieved. Wedding work is very satisfying because usually everyone is very excited and happy.

Plenty of time before the wedding, book those of the party

who want their hair styled on the day. Prioritize the bookings by starting with the bride's hair, so she has time to get ready and relax(!), then mother and bridesmaids, and finally anyone else who at the last minute may like help with such things as hats. Ask if you can have a well-lit room to yourself, out of the hustle and bustle of the rest of the wedding party, and create a little relaxed haven for your clients. Essential attributes for the hairdresser in this situation include being calm and organized, and using excellent time-management skills. When you have finished, ensure that you tidy all your equipment away quickly and leave the house as soon as possible.

The party plan

The organizing and running of hair parties is a very good way to start in business because it is an enjoyable social event and your hostess also benefits by having a free haircut or make-over. The hostess could be a member of your family or a friend who invites her friends along to her home, where they can have their hair styled on the spot or make an appointment. You must provide the 'image experience', including fashion videos and style books, whilst offering your expert advice and selling your skills and any products you have chosen. Wine and snacks or coffee and biscuits can be provided, depending on what your hostess decides is most appropriate. Parties can be held in the evening or during the day – whenever is most convenient to you and your hostess. Once your potential clients can see how good you are, you will soon have many more bookings from individuals or for hair parties.

In the workplace

Working clients can be offered a freelance hairdressing service just about anywhere, as long as you fit into their day: at home, in shops, offices or factories, there are opportunities everywhere. As part of their employee care package, large companies may be interested in offering a monthly hairdressing service. They may think it is worth encouraging their employees to be well-groomed, reflecting a smart corporate image. It helps if you have a contact in a business in order to put forward your proposal, but if you do not, all you have to do is ask.

This service may suit those individuals who do not want to waste valuable time at the weekend queuing at the barber's shop or hairdressing salon.

Hospitals and homes

In hospitals and homes you must be very flexible in adapting to potential difficulties with the washing and styling of hair, especially if the client is disabled, bedridden or cannot move very easily. Your clients could be any age with different practical constraints that need to be overcome with as little discomfort or embarrassment to them as possible. For hospital work, it is helpful if you are not the squeamish type and do not mind being near patients with different problems in a ward.

Different levels of facilities are available at different locations and it is worth checking out exactly what you will need to take before you go. It would be wise to take extra towels and gowns in case of accidental splashes of water from taps and sinks that are not designed for wheelchair users. In these situations, you should give your clients extra time if they need it, so they do not feel rushed. For hospitals and homes, it would probably be worth investing in a specially designed mobile sink to take with you.

Old people's flats

If you enjoy working with the older generation, old people's flats could be a good place to start, especially since there is a community feel about such accommodation and it is easy to get from one flat to the next. The residents of these communities are usually fairly mobile, but you still need to take your time and offer a helping hand to those who may require it. Approach the warden and ask if your services may be required.

Parent and toddler groups and playgroups

Parent and toddler groups and/or playgroups are fun if you enjoy working with children. Here you can concentrate on doing haircuts and maybe a blow-dry if clients have washed their hair beforehand (unless washing facilities are available). This idea works best if you have access to a spare room that is quieter and away from the main activities. It is also important from a safety point of view, to avoid toddlers and babies crawling through hair or slipping on any water that may have accidentally dripped on to the floor. Parents and toddlers are happy to be in a relaxed atmosphere that is designed just for them, which helps to make your job easier.

Advertise your hairdressing services with a poster or through a playgroup newsletter a few days before you are due to go in to the playgroup. Put a list of times up outside the hall so that parents or carers can book themselves or their children in by putting their names next to the time which is convenient to them. If you go regularly every five or six weeks, this service is very useful for clients to plan haircuts. Ask the playgroup leader to put your intended work dates on the term's activity calendar. You can probably negotiate a reasonable rate of commission for the use of the room, depending on who is in charge of the playgroup.

Performing groups and drama clubs

Performing groups and drama clubs always need expert help with wigs and historic hairstyles, but it may be difficult to find a company or group able to pay for your services. However, though most of this work may be voluntary, it is still a good way to get your work noticed, especially when you have your name printed in the credits on the programme.

Before a performance, be very strict about organizing your time so that you style the actors who are on stage first. You can find out the order of appearance by looking at the details from the script. This may sound very obvious, but you will discover that where some actors are more nervous than others about going on stage, they will try and pressure you into styling their hair first. It may be worth asking the director if you can have a room near the stage so that actors can find you easily and gain access to the stage quickly. Be prepared with plenty of hairgrips, hairbands and hairspray for those who forget their own, and claim back any expenses you incur through the club treasurer. Theatre work will give you a new challenge, adding to your experience – and it is fun!

Hair extensions and manicures

Hair extensions have been around for a long time, being used particularly by the Afro-Caribbean community, though now they are more widely available for all types of hair. Hair extensions allow clients to have long hair without having to wait years for it to grow by having extensions bonded to their existing hair. For details of this service contact your local wholesaler.

A large market also exists for a manicure and nail extension service, especially since more women require long-lasting, natural-looking nails. To operate this service you will need a basic knowledge of nails so you can learn extension techniques and, if necessary, identify any disorders. Details of nail extension systems and training can be found at your local wholesaler.

7 Advertising and Promoting Your Business

If potential clients do not know about you and your business, they will be unable to buy services or products from you. Therefore, you may have to promote your services through public demonstrations and advertising.

As a hairdresser you have to sell your clients a product that they have not even seen yet (as far as a change of hairstyle goes), so you must give them as close an idea as possible of what you can provide. Clients buy not only through necessity but also in response to the latest fashion, for convenience or because someone else has a hairstyle they admire. The only things a potential client has to go on are recommendations and their first contact with you, whether it is through an advert in the newspaper or a shop window, over the telephone or by meeting you personally; therefore, first impressions really count in the way you present yourself and your business.

You must decide what kind of public image you would like to project to your potential clients. In many ways, this is possibly the most enjoyable part of starting up in business. You can have great fun deciding when, how and where to advertise your services, what kind of business card and price list to have printed and whether or not to have a special logo. A logo can be a sign, picture, symbol or your business name written in special lettering, which can be put on to your stationery, transport, products and uniform, and which clients recognize as your trademark.

Your personal appearance is also very important because clients have expectations of how they think you ought to look and will feel more comfortable in the presence of someone they can identify with. Should you wear jeans and T-shirt? Or should you wear a suit? Whatever you decide, keep your figure in mind all the time and make fashion work for you.

Selecting a uniform

If you are short your aim will be to look taller, so avoid outfits that have pleated skirts, large belts and three-quarter-length sleeves. Choose shoes that have a low front without a bar or strap across the foot, because this appears to shorten legs. Keep the same colour at the hem as at the shoulder and, if you prefer to wear trousers, give the illusion of height by using the same principle. If you are tall, you may be tempted to slouch to appear shorter; instead, keep shoulders back and enjoy being able to wear most outfits!

From your initial client market research, you should gain a good idea of what kind of business image will be best and most suitable. Choose a colour scheme for your business and make sure it is one that suits you well. Coordinate your clothes, equipment and transport to match and tone. The effect of this will convey a professional image to your clients.

Your attitude is also very important, if you are to be successful. Make sure that you are always friendly, well-mannered and able to communicate with the many different kinds of clients you are likely to meet. Always listen to your clients and let them lead the conversation. Never gossip about other people, hairdressers, salons or haircuts in a derogatory way because, instead of making you look better, this will cause clients to wonder whether you might say similar things about them.

Choosing a name for your business

When choosing the right name for your business, you must

take into consideration whether you think the name may date your business or fail to reflect the image you are trying to promote. To help you with some ideas for choosing a name, here is a list of possibilities:

Hair Mobile	Hair Jalopy	Stage Coach	AutoHairStop
FirstCall A1 Hair	New Concept	First Choice	Circles
Roundabout	Solo	Step Ahead	Zigzag
Formula 1	Car'n'Clippers	Travel'n'Trim	Head First
Miles Ahead	Hair Tiz	ClubCut	Head over Wheels
ExclusiveHair	Fanny Adams	HeadHunter	Head of Hair
Headway	Petite Salon	PowerCuts	Salon Saloon
New Wave	Car Style	Beauty Car	Classic Cuts
Fresh Hair	The Cutter	HairDirector	Get Set
Hair about Town	Impulse	Headmaster	Head Girl
Heads You Win	Headstart		

Simply Red [whatever your car colour]
The Curl Specialist [or Colour etc.]
Just Jane [or whatever your name is]
Pat on the Head [if Pat is your name!]
Hair by [your name]
[Your name] for Hair

Designing a logo

Designing your business logo should be a much simpler task after you have decided upon a colour scheme and business name, and the image you want to project. Experiment with different kinds of lettering, images or shapes you think may look effective. Look in the Yellow Pages for ideas of typefaces and graphics. There is a wealth of ideas all around you, so make mental notes of things which catch your eye and try to use a similar format in your design. Keep your designs simple.

Offer a selection of designs to your family and friends and ask them what they think, then choose the logo which you prefer and can easily have reproduced on all your promotional material.

The first item on which you will present your name and logo to the world will be your business card, which should be printed in the standard size so that it can be fitted easily into clients' purses or wallets to avoid loss. Other places you may wish to display your business name or logo include:

- the local press
- your local newsagent's window
- the side of your car
- your style book
- your price list
- your uniform (if you choose to have one)
- letter headings
- towels and gowns
- styling products
- magazine folders and haircare leaflets

The cost of a basic business stationery pack, available from a national printer, is around £60 and this comprises one hundred of each of the following: A4 letterheads; compliment slips; business cards; plain envelopes. Alternatively, if you do all your own artwork on your PC and place four copies on A4 paper, one hundred business cards can be photocopied on to card for just £10.

Using a style book

Your style book is probably your most useful aid in helping to sell your services. The following is a list of suggestions on its presentation and items you may wish to include in it:

- Use a wallet-style book which has plastic inserts; this looks very professional and neat.
- Present as many styles as possible in an attractive way.
- Use colour pictures because this promotes hair colouring, and it makes selection easier for clients who are looking for different effects for their hair.
- Even if there is not a style exactly like the one the

87

client has in mind, use the style book to clarify such issues as length of hair or tightness of curl.

- Psychologists tell us that some people think in pictures while others think in words. The 'word' people may benefit from a prompt list of hairstyle descriptions to choose from, giving them an opportunity to express themselves better. A list of descriptions you could use in your list might include:

Youthful	Short	Straight	Back
Sporty	Very short	Curly	Forward
Glamorous	Long	Wavy	Manageable
Serious	Layered	Classic	Contrived
Frivolous	Fringe	Coloured	High
Smart	Half fringe	Lighter	Flat
Romantic	Ears showing	Darker	Feathery
Sexy	Ears hidden	Highlights	Thick
Fun	One length	Lowlights	Unusual
Natural	Fashionable	Shoulder length	

- Include interesting features from glossy magazines, such as 'What face shape have I?' and so on. Change these features frequently to keep your clients' interest.
- Include 'before' and 'after' photographs of your own work.
- Present your price list in an attractive, easily understandable way, aiming the format at your chosen type of client.
- Include copies of your hard-earned hairdressing certificates.
- When using your style book, listen to your clients. Talking about different options and really getting to know what they want will give them satisfaction and confidence in you.

Using your own photographs

The photographs taken to go into your style book require

thought and a good-quality, clear result. The importance of adding existing clients to the style book cannot be underestimated, especially if they are well known within the community. Most cameras nowadays are foolproof and do produce good results. However, other aspects should be considered to ensure that you reach an acceptable standard. Remember, each photograph is a tool which will encourage the client to buy services and products from you.

'Before' and 'after' photographs are a good idea and accentuate improvements for your client. For the 'before' picture, prepare the model by combing the hair in a different way so as to contrast it with the finished style. For example, if the hair is to look smooth in the final picture, then tousle the hair and if it is to look tousled in the finished picture, smooth it! If your model is female, ask her to remove cosmetics so she does not look too made-up.

For simplicity, avoid using a flash (unless you are confident about getting excellent results) because this can cause unwanted shadows and make your model's face look pale. It is better, if possible, to use natural light near a bright window or, if it is not too windy or wet, to pose your model outside. Be aware of the background and composition of your photograph. A fussy, patterned wallpaper or objects that appear to be growing out of your model's head will cause distraction and look peculiar, whereas a plain background will focus the eye on the hairstyle! If your model has blonde hair, choose a dark background and vice versa as this will create a contrast and look more effective. When taking portraits, always focus on the eyes and try to fill the frame with only the head and shoulders of your model. Remember, the purpose of the 'before' photograph is to aim for an overall effect that is asking to be bettered; while the 'after' photograph should show a definite improvement, with the model looking happier and more colourful with a touch of make-up applied.

Once you have styled the hair to a high standard and it has been groomed perfectly, you could ask your model to change into another outfit which flatters the hairstyle. If the model is a man and you have given him a short, classic style, then a sporty outfit would look good. Alternatively, for a lady, a glamorous effect is usually appreciated, with make-up that accentuates the eyes and lips applied. An off-the-shoulder top usually looks flattering, and perhaps a fine necklace and suitable earrings could be added to complete the effect. Pose your model in front of a suitable background as before, experimenting to find the most flattering position and using the viewfinder of your camera as a frame to check your composition.

Another business opportunity could arise when your models like their photographs so much that they want to buy copies for themselves. Be prepared for this and work out beforehand a list of reasonable charges for reprints, enlargements and framing.

Carry your camera with you everywhere, so that you can take photos of your own work. If you see a hairstyle you like on someone you do not know, ask the wearer if you can take a photo! Good places to see many different hairstyles are holiday resorts where people have come from all over the world; it is always interesting to see the styles other hairdressers are creating.

Presenting your price list

Your price list should be freely available to clients and displayed at or near the beginning of your style book – never hidden away. Clients should always have the opportunity to check your prices without being embarrassed by having to ask you all the time.

If there is an obvious theme in the business name you have chosen, use it to make your price list look more attractive. Here is an example of a traditional format:

	£
Wet cut	5.00
Blow-dry	5.00

However, it could be made to look more interesting than this, especially for children and teenagers. Why not copy the format of popular restaurants by using coloured pictures and different typefaces, making up your own names for different services, such as Velvet Waves, Colour Cocktails, Glamour Curl, Red Lights and Mini-cuts for children. Pay special attention to the layout by literally cutting, placing and pasting sections of the price list on to a large piece of plain paper, experimenting with different positions and artwork. Make it fun for clients to choose services you are offering. Remember, the more you offer the more you will sell.

You should, as a freelance hairdresser, be aware of the market potential of hairdressing products and tailor your services accordingly. There may be all sorts of extras that could boost your turnover. As well as selling your hairdressing and beauty services, you could sell a range of hair and beauty products. Costing retail items is a matter of taking the cost price and adding a mark-up of at least fifty per cent. If you want to expand the retail side of your business, you could sell:

- Jewellery, perhaps in conjunction with ear-piercing
- Cosmetics
- Health products
- Clothes
- Hair products, such as shampoos, conditioners, brush sets and hair ornaments

Take photographs of your products and show clients a catalogue, but make sure you have confidence in the products you are selling. Think about using own-brand packaging: it looks most professional. Look in the Yellow Pages for packaging specialists or ask your local wholesaler, who may be able to help you.

It is important at all times to keep your eyes open for new business opportunities, combining your hairdressing skills and business acumen. You can look for ways of increasing profitability by doing what you do now but even better.

Selling styling products

As a hairdresser you are selling all the time, but a few further pointers may help you when selling retail products. Selling for yourself requires confidence; there are three keys to success:

1. Be prepared.
2. Know what to say and when to say it.
3. Sell!

It is easier to sell on a one-to-one basis, allowing you to develop your skills gradually and to 'grow', perhaps selling your products to larger groups of people. Have a comprehensive product book that is very attractive to your clients, with prices which are easy to read. Outline your objectives each time you visit a client; for example if you are booked to do a perm, introduce your client to other products and services after you have finished treating the hair. Create a selling campaign for a whole year; you could promote health products in the spring, conditioning treatments during the summer and gift ideas in the winter.

Involving your client

It is always a good idea to get your client involved by using samples of your products; this will increase interest and the likelihood of sales. Samples could include conditioners and special shampoos. Photographs of your work will also show clients what you can actually do and will gain their attention. In addition, leave something with your client, such as a sample or a price list; this will reinforce what you have told them.

Your aim is to keep your customers so satisfied that they ask you to return. This can be done by pitching your approach and greeting at the right level and tone for each individual client. Find out the kinds of things your clients are interested in by really listening to them. Present your services and products effectively via your style book and use additional techniques, such as hair-storming and finding the performance point (see below) of your clients' hair.

Hair-storming

Hair-storming is similar to the technique of brainstorming and you can use this method to develop a new hairstyle relatively quickly for a client who is not sure what style to have.

If the hair is wet, comb it around the head, changing partings and hair directions and making the shape suit the individual features of your client or model. If the hair is dry, repeat as for wet hair. In addition, you have the extra dimension of height and volume, which can be introduced by back-combing the hair. At this stage, all the working should be quite rough, producing an impression of the final look. The only rules that should be applied to this method are that no ideas are to be criticized and that all the most suitable aspects of the hair-storm are remembered and then used to form part of the final hairstyle.

Assessing the performance point

The performance point is a very useful idea: it is the point at which your hair is doing exactly what you want it to do – the perfect length. Ask your client to make a note of the exact time when this point occurs. From this date one can plan ahead to a forthcoming event and cut or treat the hair at the optimum time, so that it looks perfect on the big day.

Closing the sale

The moment when the client agrees to buy your skills or styling products from you should always be a relaxed, natural affair. Closing the sale would follow a question like, 'Shall I make your appointment for your perm now?' or 'What type of hairspray would you like?'

Keeping your clients

Clients need the reassurance that they can contact you at any time for advice on handling their new perm or haircut; this is a major component of client satisfaction. A good way to do this to give your clients advice and tips as you are styling their hair, demonstrating exactly what needs to be done to achieve the best finished result. This will boost confidence and help clients to manage styles when you are not there. In addition, you could leave an information leaflet as a reminder of the points you have covered; the example below could be given to clients who want more general hair advice and information about what is available:

Your hair is one of the first things other people will notice about you. Follow these simple steps and make the most of yourself!

- Wash your hair regularly with a good-quality shampoo and conditioner [insert the name of the products you are selling here] *before* it looks greasy.
- Have you hair trimmed every six weeks to keep it in shape and looking healthy (on average, your hair grows just over a centimetre a month).
- Don't forget that if you feel like a change, having your hair cut is merely one option. Why not try a [insert product name] perm to make your hair look wavy or curly, or have a colour put on to liven it up. Choose from temporary, semi-permanent or permanent colours.
- Temporary colours include coloured setting mousse or toner sachets, such as [insert product names], which are removed after one wash; semi-permanent colours include [insert product names], which wash out in six to eight shampoos; permanent colours include tints, highlights and bleaching, all of which stay in the hair until it grows out. Henna is another permanent colour, which builds up on the hair with each application.

When choosing a new hairstyle, ask your hairdresser for

advice – she will be delighted to help you. Please contact:
Carmen Curl
Tel.: 01592 873007

This information could be given after a perm:

Congratulations on your new [insert name of product] perm!

- Your perm should last you approximately [insert duration].
- Your first wash should be preferably one week after your appointment date, to give your hair the opportunity to 'harden' in its new shape.
- For best results use [insert product name] shampoo and conditioner.
- Your first trim should be four to six weeks after your perm, the effect of which will be to revitalize your curls.
- To prevent damage try and let your hair dry naturally and finish off gently with a hairdryer or diffuser.

If you have any problems at all, please do not hesitate to contact:
Carmen Curl
Tel.: 01592 873007

8 Public Demonstrations

Public demonstrations are the most effective way of showing potential clients how good you are at hairdressing, giving customers confidence in you before they commit themselves to an appointment. Each demonstration is therefore special because the way you look and what you say and do are very visible and it is crucial to get your performance right. The following are four types of public demonstration:

Women's groups

Women's groups are constantly looking for speakers who will inform and entertain them for an hour or so. Beauty subjects are always popular and you could talk about your speciality, such as perming or cutting, or whatever subject you feel most comfortable with. However, make-overs are probably the easiest of beauty aspects to cover because you can talk through what you are doing and reveal some tricks of the trade. Preparation is the key to a successful talk. The five main points to consider are:

1. the aims and objectives of the talk
2. the audience's requirements
3. the appropriateness of the talk
4. the location of the talk
5. the seating plan

The aims and objectives of the talk should be discussed with the organizer first to ensure they are relevant to the particular age range and interests of your audience; for example, your talk on special party make-up effects will not be very useful to a group of ladies whose average age is seventy. More suitable subjects may be skincare or low-maintenance hairstyles. Find out exactly how long your talk should last and plan the order and timing of each part; for example, if your talk is to take thirty minutes and the subject is 'Easy-care Hairstyles', your plan may look something like this:

8.00   Introduce theme.
8.05   Briefly look at the full range – show slides.
8.10   Go through a smaller, more specific selection of slides and explain how effects are achieved, noting their advantages and disadvantages.
8.25   Finish and thank audience for their attention. Any questions?

It is advisable to visit the hall where you are going to give your talk to find out how it is set up and where the electrical sockets are, in case you need them. The size of the group and the acoustics of the hall will dictate whether or not you need a microphone. In some halls you may find what is known as a 'loop system'. This benefits the hard-of-hearing as the sound is transmitted from the microphone straight to hearing-aids which have been switched to the 'T' position. However, the system is only as good as the person using it because, if the speaker moves away from the microphone, the sound will fade and communication will be impaired.

Plan the seating so that everyone will be able to see and hear you and use any desired visual aids, such as a slide- or overhead projector.

The presentation

Your delivery of the presentation must be clear and easy to understand. Do not talk too quickly and be sure to accentuate important points. Your body language is also something you must be aware of. An open, relaxed posture rather than hunched back and crossed arms will make you look confident and improve your speaking. Try not to talk with your hands because this can be distracting. Instead, either clasp your hands together or put one hand in a hip-pocket. Wear a smart but comfortable outfit: not one which you are forever pulling down self-consciously. Make sure any equipment you are going to use works and is ready to switch on. Don't forget to smile!

General demonstration tips

- Be prepared – make a plan and work out how long each aspect of your demonstration will take. Remember all the equipment you are going to use on the night. If you have a model and you are going to demonstrate a haircut, ask him or her to have clean hair before demonstration so that all you have to do is damp it down with a water spray.
- Have a trial run with your model, if possible, so you can get to know both the model and his or her hair. The demonstration organizer will probably be able to find you a model from the group – there are usually lots of volunteers!
- Don't be over-adventurous with your demonstration. If you are styling hair, keep it simple.

Craft fairs

Craft fairs provide a good opportunity for you to advertise both yourself and your skills. When you see an advert for a craft fair, ring up for details. Find out how much space you will have and the cost of the pitch.

The display

Most craft fairs are held inside at hotels, halls, etc., so there is no problem in setting up a stall with a display of photographs of your work and samples of your styling products, if you sell any. Display is important to any business and is an essential part of sales promotion which you can't afford to neglect. The object of the display is to attract clients and, by so doing, to increase business; the main purpose is to create new sales opportunities – to increase impulse purchases and to make sales that might otherwise have gone to competitors. Craft fairs are a particularly good place to promote specialist services, such as wedding work.

When you are planning any display, keep the following principles in mind:

1. Preparation
2. Space
3. Layout
4. Design
5. Colour
6. Lighting

A good display establishes contact with potential clients. It reflects the character of your business, helps to publicize the services offered and builds up goodwill. Prepare 'before' and 'after' pictures, which are always very effective from a central position, for example near the entrance of the fair to attract the eye of the arriving customers. It is preferable to include in your line-up of displayed photographs any models who are well-known local personalities and who have had their hair styled by you. This could be the postman or the friendly person who serves at the local newsagent. They will be flattered to have been asked to model for you, free of charge of course!

The display and demonstration must catch a potential client's attention; it is particularly effective when the view comes as a surprise. Place products and photographs in the line of the eye with further photographs at the back, placed slightly higher to create an effect that seems to cascade down to the front where you will be working. Avoid overcrowding your display and eliminate unnecessary clutter, as it bewilders the passer-by.

Good design is the essence of display: without it, no display can accomplish its purpose. If you are preparing to present your work in a hotel, the size and shape of the room must be considered. Lighting should enhance the presentation of your products, hairstyles and their colour. Design creates an audience, holds its attention and links together all the elements that make up a promotion.

Car boot sales

Car boot sales are very effective places to promote your business (if this is permissible in your area). There is only one drawback – the weather! Demonstrations at such sales are most effective in the still, warm days of summer, making it a pleasure for everyone participating.

Set up your stall using the back of your car; a hatchback is best but you can improvise if you do not have one. Use the boot to display your certificate, mirror and equipment. Everything the client can see should look spotlessly clean and tidy. Be seen to conform to the highest hygiene standards by using disinfectant to clean your equipment. Put some plastic sheeting down (approximate size 2.5×2.5 m). Not only does this mark out your territory but it is also easy to sweep clean. Two chairs should be sufficient: one for clients to wait for your services and one for your client. Set out a small table for magazines and your stylebook. Even when you are out of doors, it is important you provide these little extras!

A clear price list and business cards should be readily available for people to take. At a car boot sale you will find that once you have styled your first client's hair you will be busy the whole time. Your clients are not only the visitors to the sale but also the stallholders who will have been watching you very carefully.

Competition work

Although competition work is not strictly a direct way of promoting your business, there are other benefits. Entering competitions can be a very exciting and rewarding activity, especially if you get placed. If you win a hairdressing competition, you are likely to get your name and probably your photograph in the local paper. This will confirm to existing clients that you really are a good hairdresser and it will create interest in your business.

However, even if you do not win a competition, additional benefits include having contact with other hairdressers and keeping up with fashion trends. With new ideas, your work will be kept up to a very high standard. All this directly affects your clients and helps you to keep them.

The National Hairdressing Federation and companies such as L'Oreal and Wella hold competitions around the country, and details of these can be found in the hairdressing trade magazines. Although regulations restrict entry to certain events, anyone can enter open competitions. Contact the organizers to get details of rules, entry fees and lists.

If you have not entered a competition before or for a long time, it is worth attending one first to get a feel for what is required. If this is not possible, you will probably find videos of previous technical college competitions in the college library; these may be useful. In addition, the most recent and back issues of trade magazines are full of colour photographs of hairstyles and you should scan these for ideas.

The first factor you will have to consider before entering a competition is time: when will you and your model be able to get together to practise? You must commit yourself to the discipline of practising the same style over and over again until it is perfect.

Choosing a model

When you enter a competition, your model 'sells' the

hairstyle to the judges. Therefore, it is worth finding the right person to do the job. The qualities you are looking for in a model should include someone with the right attitude, the right looks and a fantastic wardrobe!

The right attitude to modelling is important because your model must be willing to have her hair styled in the way *you* wish. This is really the only time a hairdresser has a free hand, though of course you must still respect your model's feelings and come to an agreement at the outset on all the different aspects of modelling and each of your expectations of the venture. Your model meanwhile must enjoy having her hair styled and be patient whilst you develop your creation.

The way your model and her hair look will probably attract you to her in the first place. Blondes and redheads stand out in a crowd and on the competition floor. If possible, choose a model with fair hair as this will give you a good base to work on. Be realistic before you ask your potential model if she would like the job. For example, if you see a stunning blonde with fabulous thick hair down to her waist, it is unlikely that she will want her hair cut short into a bob (or indeed that you would want to cut it!). It is to your advantage if your model's hair is slightly wavy and bends the way you want it – and *stays* there.

The most attractive and suitable outfit is often found in the model's own wardrobe. However, if this is not the case, money can be saved on hire charges by making simple adaptations and additions to existing outfits. If you want a fantastic evening gown or period effect, a visit to your local charity shop may be the key to an economical ensemble.

As well as practising your perfect hairstyle, have at least one full dress rehearsal (timed, if possible) before the competition to ensure that you have everything to hand and that the finished total look is acceptable to you. Check that the make-up is appropriate for the look you require and always accentuate the eyes because, in addition to everything else, they will help draw the judges' attention to your model. Ensure your hairstyle is technically correct by checking to see that any partings are perfectly straight and clean and that no hair is out of place. Attention to detail at this stage is paramount. Try not to use too much hairspray or gloss because it is difficult to make improvements if the hair is too stiff. Also, if the hair is too heavy it will pull the style down rather than hold it in place.

The competition

If necessary, warn your model that she may have to travel to the competition in her rollers and hairnet. This does not pose too much of a problem if you go by car but it may be a little embarrassing on public transport, so provide a scarf or hood. Arrive at the competition venue in plenty of time and ensure your model has any refreshment she requires, apart from alcohol!

During the competition, keep calm and raise your model's confidence by complimenting her. When posing your model, the aim is to attract attention to her. This can be done by pulling her chair slightly away from the table and positioning her so that she takes up as much space as possible on the floor (without of course tripping up the judges!). Sit her on the chair at an angle, with perhaps one hand on her hip. Her head should be tilted to show off the hairstyle in its best light – but bear in mind that the position must be comfortable, because she will have to sit for about half an hour while the judging is being carried out.

Whether or not you are successful in gaining a place, it is always important to thank your model for her help when the competition is over. After all, you could not have entered without her! If she is particularly good, it may be worth asking if she would like to work with you again. As a thank-you present, you could offer your model a keepsake, in the form of a framed photograph of her taken during the competition.

9 Business Development Options

As a freelance hairdresser you can do as much or as little as you wish, depending on how ambitious you are. You can either work a few hours a week, fitting other commitments and interests into your life, or go full-time and expand your business. In the latter case, a number of options can be pursued. Five of them are introduced generally here, though more information should be sought before any individual project is undertaken. You may wish to consider the following:

- Adding a beauty and/or 'total image' service to your existing hairdressing services.
- Enlisting other hairdressers and beauticians to make your freelance business larger.
- Franchising.
- Training other hairdressers and beauticians.
- Designing hairdressing or beauty accessories.

Adding a beauty/'total image' service

Whilst training, many hairdressers also have the opportunity to learn how to become a beauty therapist and it is possible to offer your clients such services as manicures, pedicures, facials, waxing and make-up; these can be presented in the same way as your hairdressing, via your style book or in a separate book or folder.

To reflect the beauty services you are offering, you may wish to adapt or change your business name. Here are some suggestions: Top-to-Toe, Beauty Box, Beauty Concepts, Hair and Beauty Mobile, Hair and Beauty Solutions, A1 Hair and Beauty, Personal Hair and Beauty Consultant, Profiles, Mobile Image-Select.

When presenting details of beauty services, use a similar approach to that in your style book. Coloured 'before and after' photographs are always very effective when showing improvements achieved by using make-up. Beauty products can be photographed individually to maximize impact, accompanied by a description of benefits for clients. A sample price list can be found in Appendix 3.

Being able to offer more services will be very convenient for clients such as the bride-to-be or those who wish to have make-up lessons in the privacy of their own home. Your profits should increase because you can potentially make fewer visits, saving time and money.

Beauty equipment and stock checklist

Here is a general checklist to serve as a reminder of items you will need to take with you for facials, manicures, pedicures and depilatory waxing:

Facial
Gown for client and overall for yourself
Towels and blanket
Portable couch
Headband
Infra-red lamp or cool steamer
Comedone blackhead extractors
Cleansing cream
Cleansing milk
Aromatherapy oil/massage cream
Eye make-up remover
Skin tonic

Mask
Moisturizer
Spatula
Orange stick
Cotton buds
Cotton wool
Tissues
Small bowl
Mask brush
Plastic bag for waste
Plastic bag for used equipment

Manicure
Overall for yourself
Two towels
Manicure bowl
Long emery boards
Hand cream
Nail enamel remover
Repair kit for nails/nail extension kit
Base/top coat
Nail enamel
Drying spray
Cotton wool
Liquid soap
Small nail-brush
Cuticle massage cream
Cuticle remover
Cuticle knife
Buffing cream
Buffer
Orange stick
Rubber hoof stick
Plastic bag for waste
Plastic bag for used equipment

Pedicure
Gown for client and overall for yourself

Two towels
Foot bath
Long emery boards
Hand cream
Nail enamel remover
Base/top coat
Nail enamel
Drying spray
Cotton wool
Liquid soap/antiseptic
Small nail-brush
Cuticle massage cream
Cuticle remover
Cuticle knife
Hard skin remover
Buffing cream
Buffer
Orange stick
Rubber hoof stick
Plastic bag for waste
Plastic bag for used equipment

Depilatory Waxing
Gown for client and overall for yourself
Towels
Portable couch
Thermostatically controlled heater
Wax
Polythene sheeting and couch paper
Spirit solution
Brush (to apply wax)
Cotton strips
Antiseptic soothing lotion
Tissues
Tweezers
Plastic bag for waste
Plastic bag for used equipment

Make-up
Gown for client and overall for yourself
Two towels
Headband
Cleansing cream
Cleansing milk
Skin toner
Moisturizer
Tweezers
Make-up
Mirror
Eyelash curler
Cotton wool
Tissues
Plastic bag for waste
Plastic bag for used equipment

Another idea would be not only to combine hairdressing and beauty but also to advise on the best colours and outfits for different occasions. Clients may want to change or update their whole image generally or to look particularly smart for an important interview or occasion. Courses on colour are widely available and books on the subject can be found in libraries and bookshops.

Making your business larger

As there is a limit to the number of clients you can service, you can enlist other hairdressers to cover the extra work load. Each hairdresser pays you an agreed sum of money each week and in return you find work for them. Start with one hairdresser and increase the number as demand dictates.

A central control should be set up to monitor all appointments, and work is then offered to hairdressers who are on your books. To start with, the control could be yourself whilst you are out working, or at your home. If the business becomes successful, a full-time receptionist could be employed to take appointments. It is advantageous to have another hairdresser as a central control in order to offer advice to other team members; it is always comforting to know that there is someone available to talk to about hairdressing and business matters.

All hairdressers should be fully qualified and have their own transport and equipment, thus keeping standards high. They should also specify times when they are able to work for the central control in their preferred area. Stock should be held at the control for purchase by the team at reasonable rates (because of economies of scale), thereby saving hairdressers time and money having to buy it themselves. If by chance an unexpected sale is made, stock can then be taken direct to the client.

There is scope within this business idea to offer clients a high-quality, more flexible service, perhaps operating from 7 a.m. until 9 p.m. seven days a week. Each of the team members charges clients a standard fee, which keeps prices up, and all freelancers operate under the same business name, projecting the same corporate image.

The hairdressers you want to attract are those who enjoy working in a team and who are self-motivated but do not actually want the responsibility of advertising for themselves. An added bonus for them is that clients cannot contact them at home and so they can truly get away from work when they wish to do so.

Advice about aspects of freelancing should be given to newcomers by you and any other team members who are experienced in this field. Good management of the team is essential. Build a team and keep it motivated by observing the following:

- **Praise and thank the team for its efforts** – when the team is doing well, let its members know: if your team feels good about itself, it is likely to perform better.
- **Tell members about the business, its problems and the future** – have regular meetings and involve the team in decision-making and problem-solving.

109

- **Trust your team members; if they are occasionally a few minutes late, do not keep checking on them** – if they are late, find out why and perhaps change schedules to accommodate them.
- **Do not reprimand team members in public, especially in front of colleagues or clients** – do reprimand as soon as possible after the event, if you have to. Once you have explained the problem and how you feel about it, do not mention it again.
- **Do not have favourites** – treat everyone equally and fairly.
- **If team members do something well, make sure they get the credit** – encourage team members by praising them when they demonstrate positive attributes: action, energy, flexibility, adaptability, perseverance, tenacity and patience.
- **If team members come to you with problems, listen and show sympathy and understanding** – if they need advice, refer them to a professional who may be able to help.
- **Do not keep changing the rules** – if you have to, tell the whole team.
- **Never assume team members are wrong until you find out the facts** – be loyal to your team and it will be loyal to you.

Franchising

When your business has become well established and your operating methods are proving successful, you may wish to consider the franchising option. This means that, in exchange for fees, other suitably qualified hairdressers receive the goodwill that you have developed, your managing and marketing expertise and reduced stock costs as a result of centralized bulk buying. You would be known as a franchiser and the hairdresser buying the franchise would be known as a franchisee.

Before a franchise can be set up, the franchiser should

thoroughly test the idea for suitability by setting up and operating at least one pilot business. The franchisee is the business owner, not the franchiser, although they do rely on each other and the franchiser must continually ensure that the franchisee is carrying out the business as was originally agreed. Terms of agreement must be comprehensively described in a franchise contract, which states the methods of operation, the franchiser's obligations and the geographical area the franchisee can cover.

The British Franchise Association (BFA) is the UK franchise industry's trade organization and offers advice to both franchisers and franchisees. It has produced an information pack costing £19.50, which is available from the BFA, Franchise Chambers, 75a Bell Street, Henley-on-Thames, Oxon. RG9 2BD. Tel.: 01491 578049/50.

Training other hairdressers

There are many opportunities to train other hairdressers. You could do this in conjunction with your local wholesaler, by demonstrating and promoting its products, or you could offer short courses on hairdressing to existing training establishments, or design an adult education course for those wishing to return to hairdressing after a break.

To do this, it is essential to have a teaching qualification. Most colleges offer the Further Adult Education Teaching Certificate (FAETC) stages I and II, which are at NVQ level 3 or 4, depending on how many units are taken. It lasts for approximately one year part-time. There are no entry requirements as such, but you do need to have something to teach!

The first part of the FAETC (stage I) is an introductory course for students to find out whether teaching is for them. The course runs for ten weeks, one evening per week at most further education colleges, and costs around £70. In addition, six hours of teaching pratice must be completed. The course covers the following:

- The needs of the organization you are training for
- Students' needs
- Planning and organizing
- Teaching practice
- Preparing resources
- Teaching evaluation
- Assessing students

Stage II runs for thirty-four weeks, one evening a week, and costs around £300. The course is the same as stage I but goes into more depth, and a teaching practice portfolio has to be produced by the end of it. You will need to have completed a minimum of twenty-four hours' teaching in order to meet the assessment requirements. One advantage of doing this course is that you will build up important contacts.

Wherever you would like to teach, you must prepare a proposal similar to a business plan. You need to sell your idea to the person who decides which courses to run. First, do some market research to make sure there is suitable demand and then present the results of this and the proposed course details.

Alternatively, you could hire your own premises and run courses without having to seek permission, although you must still ensure that you are selling a worthwhile, viable course direct to your customers. As well as the cost of the premises you hire, you will have to take advertising costs into consideration. The current trainer's charge is approximately £250 per day. Your costs could be covered by charging £40 per student for a one-day course, offering ten places.

Designing hairdressing accessories

As a hairdresser you probably have a natural flair for design, bearing in mind the fact that you create original hairstyles all the time. With an eye for shape and colour, and a practical approach to problem-solving, you may have noticed difficulties that, with a bit of thought, can be resolved. New hairdressing equipment and accessories are being designed and introduced all the time to make life easier and more comfortable for the client and hairdresser alike – you too can do the same.

If you choose to try this business idea it can be very risky and expensive, especially if you need to employ others to manufacture your designs. All your acquired management skills will be necessary if you are to be successful. However, it is not unknown for designers to make their own products very reasonably from their own home and then to move a growing business to larger premises or sell the product idea if it becomes successful.

Design, like all human planning, consists of assembling information about the present state of the world around us, processing that information according to the models we have in our heads and making a plan of action for some kind of intervention in the situation. This may mean either modifying what there is at present or introducing something quite new into the situation.

Quite often a good idea is lost, either because it is not recorded when it is first thought of or because there is a belief that someone else *must* have had the same idea already. Keep a small ideas notebook handy at all times and leave it next to your bed at night, because quite often inspiration comes to you when you are relaxed and least expecting it. As freelance hairdressing is a comparatively new occupation, you have plenty of scope to think of ways of improving equipment and methods and then to put your ideas into practice.

113

Appendices

1: Example of a business plan

Carmen Curl – Freelance Hairdresser
4 The Cut
Combe Down
Somerset
Tel.: 01592 873007

Description of business
A freelance hairdresser offers every service provided by a salon but with the advantage that these services take place at the customer's home or office.

Aims
To generate sufficient revenue to provide a net income before tax of £15,000 p.a.

Market
The market exists among those unable or unwilling to go to a salon, such as mothers with young children, the disabled and those who find salon hours inconvenient. My thorough market research makes me confident that I have sufficient potential clients to trade profitably. I intend to extend my clientele by leaflet drops and local advertising and I believe that, having worked successfully in a salon in the area for some five years, personal recommendation will speedily increase my business.

Competition
There are four salons in this area but no other freelance

hairdressers. I have carefully studied hairdressing prices and am satisfied that my charges will prove highly competitive.

Operation

I shall be a sole trader under my own name, based at my home address, and shall travel by car to clients' homes, offices, etc. My telephone will be manned at all times but, if the business expands to the expected level, I shall purchase a mobile phone. All services provided by a hairdressing salon will be available from me and, in addition, I intend to carry stock for sale to customers.

Investment required

Attached are details of car, equipment and stock before business can commence, amounting to £6,993.

Bank overdraft required

Of the initial expenditure required, I have £1,000 available and therefore seek an overdraft limit of £6,000 which I will repay in two years, after which time I anticipate the business will fund itself.

Trading forecast

I attach a forecast that reveals an upward trend of profit, reflecting an enlarged clientele and increasing sales of goods.

Personal details

Particulars of relevant information are attached [Appendix 2].

EQUIPMENT	£	STOCK	£
Gowns × 3	45.00	Mousse	3.00
Scissors × 3	21.00	Hairspray	3.00
Clippers	25.00	Setting lotion	5.00
Towels	36.00	Shampoo	7.00
Hairdryers × 2	55.00	Conditioner	10.00
Combs	24.00	End papers	5.00
Curlers	30.00	Perm lotion	20.00
Tongs	20.00	Neutralizer	10.00
Hot brush	15.00	Highlight cap	10.00
Brushes × 4	15.00	Sponge	1.50
Diffuser	10.00	Cotton wool	10.00
Mirrors × 2	50.00	Plastic gloves and caps	5.00
Trolley	40.00	Bleach	15.00
Style book	10.00	Tint × 8	26.00
Bag	45.00	Peroxide	10.00
		Make-up	50.00
		Barrier cream	1.50
		Stationery	30.00
TOTAL	441.00		222.00

Items required	£
Car	4,500.00
Washing machine	230.00
Tumble dryer	100.00
Equipment	441.00
Stock	222.00
PC and printer	1,500.00
TOTAL	6,993.00

CASH FLOW FORECAST AND PROFIT PROJECTION FOR THE YEAR ENDING 31ST DECEMBER 1996

PROFIT PROJECTION

	Jan	Feb	Mar	Apr	May	Jun	Jul	Aug	Sep	Oct	Nov	Dec	TOTAL
Takings	£800.00	£800.00	£900.00	£1,000.00	£1,400.00	£1,400.00	£1,400.00	£1,400.00	£1,400.00	£1,400.00	£1,400.00	£1,400.00	£14,700.00
Less cost of stock	£222.00	£0.00	£50.00	£50.00	£70.00	£70.00	£70.00	£60.00	£150.00	£100.00	£70.00	£70.00	£982.00
GROSS PROFIT	£578.00	£800.00	£850.00	£950.00	£1,330.00	£1,330.00	£1,330.00	£1,340.00	£1,250.00	£1,300.00	£1,330.00	£1,330.00	£13,718.00
Less Expenses													
Vehicle purchase	£4,500.00	£0.00	£0.00	£0.00	£0.00	£0.00	£0.00	£0.00	£0.00	£0.00	£0.00	£0.00	£4,500.00
Motor Fuel	£40.00	£40.00	£40.00	£40.00	£40.00	£50.00	£50.00	£60.00	£60.00	£60.00	£70.00	£70.00	£620.00
Motor Tax/Insurance	£23.00	£23.00	£23.00	£23.00	£23.00	£23.00	£23.00	£23.00	£23.00	£23.00	£23.00	£23.00	£276.00
Drawings	£400.00	£400.00	£400.00	£500.00	£600.00	£700.00	£800.00	£800.00	£900.00	£900.00	£900.00	£1,000.00	£8,300.00
Electricity	£15.00	£15.00	£15.00	£15.00	£15.00	£15.00	£15.00	£15.00	£15.00	£15.00	£15.00	£15.00	£180.00
Insurance (liability)	£55.00	£0.00	£0.00	£0.00	£0.00	£0.00	£0.00	£0.00	£0.00	£0.00	£0.00	£0.00	£55.00
Professional	£10.00	£10.00	£10.00	£10.00	£10.00	£10.00	£10.00	£10.00	£10.00	£10.00	£10.00	£10.00	£120.00
Telephone	£25.00	£25.00	£25.00	£25.00	£25.00	£25.00	£25.00	£25.00	£25.00	£25.00	£25.00	£25.00	£300.00
Equipment	£761.00	£0.00	£0.00	£0.00	£0.00	£0.00	£0.00	£0.00	£0.00	£0.00	£0.00	£0.00	£761.00
Depreciation(Equip & Car)	£132.00	£132.00	£132.00	£132.00	£132.00	£132.00	£132.00	£132.00	£132.00	£132.00	£132.00	£132.00	£1,584.00
TOTAL EXPENSES	£5,961.00	£645.00	£645.00	£745.00	£845.00	£955.00	£1,055.00	£1,065.00	£1,165.00	£1,165.00	£1,175.00	£1,275.00	£16,696.00
NET PROFIT/NET LOSS	-£5,383.00	£155.00	£205.00	£205.00	£485.00	£375.00	£275.00	£275.00	£85.00	£135.00	£155.00	£55.00	-£2,968.00
CUMULATIVE TOTAL	-5,373.00	-£5,218.00	-£5,013.00	-£4,808.00	-£4,323.00	-£3,948.00	-£3,673.00	-£3,398.00	-£3,313.00	-£3,178.00	-£3,023.00	-£2,968.00	

CARMEN CURL TRADING AS CARMEN CURL INCOME AND EXPENDITURE ACCOUNT AS AT 31 DECEMBER 1996

Total Sales (takings)		14,700
Less cost of sales		
Opening stock	222	
Add purchases	972	
	1,194	
less closing stock	100	1,094
Gross profit		13,606
less expenses		
Motor fuel	620	
Motor tax and expenses	276	
Use of home as office	156	
Insurance	55	
Professional charges	120	
Telephone	300	1,527
Net profit		12,079
less depreciation		1,584
		10,495
less taxation		630
		9,865

CARMEN CURL TRADING AS CARMEN CURL FUNDS FLOW STATEMENT AS AT 31 DECEMBER 1996

Profit generated from trading operations		12,089
less:		
Drawings	8,300	
National Insurance	294	
Taxation	630	
Depreciation	1,584	
Reserves	1,281	
		12,089

119

CARMEN CURL TRADING AS CARMEN CURL
OPENING BALANCE SHEET AS AT 1 JANUARY 1996

Fixed Assets		
Motor vehicle	4,500	
Equipment	761	5,261
Current Assets		
Opening stock	222	
Cash in bank	527	749
		6,010
Liabilities		
Capital		6,010

CARMEN CURL TRADING AS CARMEN CURL
BALANCE SHEET AS AT 31 DECEMBER 1996

Fixed Assets		
Motor vehicle	4,500	
Equipment	761	
	5,261	
less depreciation	1,584	3,677
Current Assets		
Closing stock	100	
Cash in hand	25	
Cash in bank	393	518
		4,195
Liabilities		
Capital		4,195

2: Example of a curriculum vitae

Carmen Curl
4 The Cut
Combe Down
Somerset
Tel.: 01592 873007

An enterprising person with five years' hairdressing experience. Skills include communication, self-motivation and the ability to manage others.

QUALIFICATIONS   5 GCSEs
                            NVQ levels 2 and 3 in Hairdressing

COURSES   Tinting course
                            Perming course

CAREER SUMMARY
After leaving college I worked the summer at a holiday camp, allowing me to gain rapid work experience following my training. I applied and was accepted to work in a large and well-established salon in Combe Down. I worked here for five years, building up a loyal clientele, of whom some will stay with me, after which time I had enough confidence and ability to run my own freelance hairdressing business.

SKILLS SUMMARY
Enthusiasm, professional skill and a thorough understanding of business have enabled me to be successful in hairdressing.

I am also determined and versatile, looking for opportunities to develop new ideas.

Note: Your date of birth is not very important on this c.v., but if you want to include it put it near the end.

3: Sample price list of basic hairdressing and beauty services

Hairdressing

SERVICE	£
Wet cut	5.00
Restyle	7.50
Blow-dry – short hair	5.00
long hair	7.00
Shampoo and set	7.00
Body/Root perm	20.00
Standard perm	25.00
Conditioning perm	30.00
Ultra-special perm	40.00
Highlights	20.00
Tinting – full head	25.00
roots	20.00

EXTRAS

Conditioners from:	1.00
Conditioning treatments from:	5.00
Setting lotions from:	1.00
Head and neck massage	5.00

Beauty

MINI FACIAL
Using [insert product name] for thorough cleansing. The use of [insert product name]

involves deep cleansing before a combination of treatment creams, selected for your skin type, are applied beneath the [insert product name] mask which, with its gradual rise in temperature, creates a pleasant warmth, allowing the creams to penetrate while you relax.   20.00

AROMATHERAPY MASSAGE

Using a blend of essential oils, specifically selected for your individual needs.

Face and neck	10.00
Face, neck and scalp	12.00

EYES

Eyelash tinting	8.00
Eyebrow tinting	5.00
Eyelash and eyebrow tinting	11.00
Eyebrow shaping	5.00
Eyebrow tinting and shaping	9.00
Eyelash and eyebrow tinting plus eyebrow shaping	14.00

MAKE-UP

For any occasion, per session	10.00
Make-up lesson	15.00

MANICURE

A complete treatment for nails and cuticles, including hand and arm massage and nail varnish, if required.   8.00

PEDICURE

Including footbath massage, full nail and cuticle treatment, hard skin scrub, foot and leg massage and varnish, if required.   12.00

WAXING

Full leg, bikini optional	15.00
Half leg	8.00
Half leg and bikini	11.00
Bikini	5.00
Underarm	5.00

4: Common problems

Here are some common problems freelance hairdressers experience from time to time, with suggested solutions.

My hands get really dry and rough.

Here is a very simple and effective old-fashioned remedy which really works. All you need is a drop of cooking oil and a teaspoon of sugar mixed together and rubbed over your hands. This has the effect of exfoliating the skin, making the hands feel much smoother. Wash off with soap and water and feel the difference! If this treatment does not work and your hands still become red, sore and cracked, consult your doctor.

I have a client who lives in a particularly dark house. I have tried putting the light on but it is still not bright enough and does not make much difference. I need more light in which to work.

As a freelance hairdresser, there are many factors which you cannot control. However, you do have two options in this instance. The first is to ask your client if she has a brighter room in which you can work, or if there is a spare side light which you can use. It could be that your client has a sight impairment and can actually see better in subdued lighting. Take a higher wattage light bulb with you. In either case, your client will be delighted to help you since it is in her interest to do so.

Ideally, if you are tinting or lightening hair, natural light is the best kind to work in so you can assess exactly the developing colour.

I have been called to the same empty house on two occasions and I feel a bit scared and let down.

Unfortunately, when appointments are made over the telephone, you do not know who you are talking to. If you go to an appointment once and no one is there, it is quite possible that the client has forgotten and you must give them the benefit of the doubt. However, in this instance, it sounds like someone who wants to waste your time. Make a note of the address and keep it near the telephone and if you are asked to go there again – don't go!

I have several clients who do not have a shower facility and it takes ages to rinse their hair.

There is not much you can do about this except perhaps take your own shower spray and attach it to the taps. If it does not fit, the best way to save clean water when rinsing a client's hair is to fill a bowl with the rinse water and put it to one side on the draining board. From this, fill a plastic jug with clean water and use it to rinse your client's hair over the sink so that the soapy water does not contaminate your clean supply. This method should save you some time and effort.

I visit a nice family and do all their hair. I have really enjoyed my visits – until the last time when the husband started to say suggestive things to me. I felt really embarrassed and I tried to laugh it off, but I would prefer it if he stopped saying those things.

If the husband starts embarrassing you again, without smiling you must ask him to stop. This should be enough to deter him. However, if this does not work, threaten to tell his wife. If this tactic fails, you will have to make excuses and not return. Unfortunately in cases like this, if the wife finds out about her husband's behaviour, you may be blamed for leading him on. This does not sound fair, but in order to preserve your good reputation you must move on.

I live in a large town where some road names sound similar and despite using a good street map I have still managed to go to the wrong address. This makes me late for appointments and I know it looks unprofessional.

When a client rings up for an appointment, clarify the exact location of the address by taking directions. This should solve your problem at the outset.

Ever since I trained as a hairdresser, I have styled my friends' and family's hair free of charge. Now I am in business, they expect the same treatment, but if I want to make my living from this business, how can I?

The simple answer is you can't as long as you are giving a free service. It is a big problem when making the transition from hobby to business, but it is up to you to let everyone know you are professional and ask for their support. Over a period of time you will find that your time constraints will increase and energy levels decrease, and you probably will not be inclined to give free haircuts. Do not vary the prices you charge, otherwise you will always be undercutting yourself, and do not let anyone 'settle up at the end of the week'.

How much float should I take?

First of all, charge for everything to the nearest £1 or 50p so you do not have to delve around for change. I would take a £20 float to be on the safe side, split into a £10 note, £5 note, 4 × £1 coins and 2 × 50p pieces. You can always get more change between clients, if necessary.

I have been a freelance hairdresser for a while now and I love my work, but sometimes I feel quite isolated.

You would think that because you are with people all day, a sense of isolation would not be a problem. However, because you are a professional, you cannot share your experiences with clients unless it is appropriate. I suggest you contact other freelance hairdressers like yourself, to swap stories and experiences. Do this by collecting names from adverts in the local paper or newsagents. Ring round and organize a meeting; they will appreciate your efforts!

My bank returned my client's cheque to me 'through lack of funds'. How should I get my money?

I am sure this mistake was caused through an oversight on the part of your client. If you have the client's number, ring and explain the situation and agree a time when you can collect the cash. If you can't make contact by telephone, you will have to write a note. Failing that, you will have to go round to the house. If it was not an oversight, then you have a choice: you can decide either to write off the debt and blacklist the client or to visit the Citizens' Advice Bureau for help on what to do next.

When I come home after a long day at work, I do not always feel like taking all my equipment and stock out of my car, which is parked on my drive. Surely it will be safe out there?

If you think you are too tired to empty your car, your only

option is to park it inside a locked garage. Failing to do so means that you are open to theft from opportunists, who can get into your car within seconds and take everything.

If you lose all your equipment through theft, no business can be done until you replace it. It is also extremely inconvenient, as you will have the police to contact and then all the insurance forms to fill out. A car alarm will deter the criminal but it is better and far less inconvenient for *you* to empty your car rather than them.

I have one or two clients who only contact me when they have over-processed their hair and need it sorting out. After I have 'patched up' their hair by giving it a good cut and blow-dry, it looks fine but in the meantime they put perms and tints on their hair themselves and it looks terrible. I am worried they will tell everyone I am their hairdresser and I will lose clients.

I can understand how you feel and you have two options. The first is to carry on styling your clients' hair, because you are obviously liked. The second is to put your client off politely.

If you choose the first option you could take the opportunity to give advice on the best way to care for hair and also offer information on when and how to apply tints and perms. This way clients have the benefit of some of your expertise and can help themselves to look better as well as saving your reputation. To put your mind at rest about your reputation, anyone who is friendly with your client is likely to know that she likes to 'play' with her hair and will know the difference when it has been styled by a professional – yourself!

Encourage your client to have a smart haircut which only needs trimming and looks good without perming. Your client will listen to you if what you are saying makes sense to her and the results give her positive feedback from her friends and family.

Alternatively, if you really do not think this strategy will

129

work or your client continues to mistreat her hair, explain tactfully when you are next called that your books are now full and you will not be able to help her.

My client's white hair is resistant to tint and the last time I coloured her hair, I left the tint on the hair a little longer than usual to make sure all of the white hair was covered. When I had rinsed and dried her hair, I was dismayed to notice the roots were slightly lighter than I wanted them to be. I can't understand what went wrong.

If you used the same tint and strength of peroxide as last time, there can only be one explanation; because you left the tint on longer than usual, you over-processed it. The peroxide had a slight bleaching effect and reduced the artificial colour agent.

If white hair is resistant to tint, you have three other options you can try: if you feel the tone of the tint seems correct, then either brush or dab 3% peroxide with cotton wool on to the resistant hair. This will soften the hair cuticle before you apply the tint, allowing the colour into the hair; if you think the tint chosen was too ash, choose a warmer shade; try a deeper shade of tint and a stronger volume of peroxide (no stronger than 12%), which will also soften the hair cuticle and allow effective colouring.

I visited a very nice client who had her hair permed. She seemed to like it very much and as usual I told her that she should let me know of any problems within the first week so that I could come back immediately and rectify the situation. After one week, I had a telephone call from my client, who said she thought that one side had dropped. I offered to re-perm it immediately. However, my client said she was not available for another *three* weeks. When I returned, I checked the perm and put two perm curlers in the side. My client then asked me to re-perm the whole top, because since it had been

permed it had dropped slightly. I felt very embarrassed because I felt that if there had been a real problem she would have preferred a re-perm as soon as possible in the first place. I advised her that if I re-permed the hair that had taken well, the condition would suffer. The client reluctantly accepted this, but I felt she was still not happy. Could I have handled this better?

Without actually being there, it is difficult to assess the situation properly but, as you say, three weeks is a long time to put off an appointment to fix a problem. I think you were correct not to treat hair that did not need re-perming; if you had re-permed it, your client might still have been unhappy. She might also have told all her friends how bad you are and you would have had to refund her money after having wasted another two hours.

If a similar situation arises again, fix the problem and, if your client is still not happy, refund her money immediately. That way your client will respect your judgement and hopefully not complain about you and damage your reputation.

I have an elderly client who lives alone and I do not think she has many visitors. When I visit, she makes a fuss of me and loves to show me old photographs of her family or her well-tended garden. I always end up staying longer than I planned. Last time I was late for my next appointment, but I do not know how to get away without hurting her feelings.

Yes, this must be a problem for you. Your client sounds lonely and clearly enjoys showing you things she is proud of. Boost her confidence by praising her efforts and give her plenty of opportunity to talk whilst you are styling her hair. Perhaps your client does not realize just how busy you are, so next time you visit, keep a close eye on the time and when it is time to go, explain you have another client waiting. Thank her very much for her kindness, let her know you are looking forward to your next visit and leave.

I have a client who is very unhappily married and told me that her husband is always coming home drunk. She told me that one night when he returned home and fell asleep, she tried to 'smother' him with her pillow. She felt sure that she had killed him because he stopped snoring and she pushed him out of bed. When he hit the floor he started to snore again. I was shocked to hear this story and was not sure whether to tell the police.

Clients tell freelance hairdressers all sorts of very personal things, particularly because they are in their own home and they know the information is confidential. Sometimes clients say things just for a reaction or to get something 'off their chest', without meaning too much by it and probably quickly forgetting what they have said; they would probably be mortified if hairdressers repeated any of it to them at a later date.

However, if you thought for a moment that someone's life was in danger, you would be duty-bound as a member of the public to pass information on to the police without being held liable. It is a criminal offence to threaten to harm someone. Only professionals, such as medical practitioners and solicitors, have the right to keep information completely confidential.

In this case, because you know your client's husband is still alive, you need not tell anyone, but if you still feel concerned, you should talk to someone you can trust, for your own reassurance.

How do I know how well my business is doing? I do not think my business is making enough money.

Your original business plan contains goals you have set for yourself and, if you diligently keep up your accounts or spreadsheet, you will be able to assess at a glance whether you are achieving your planned targets. Targets need not be purely financial; you could have a goal of a certain number of products for sale or a certain number of clients by a set date. However, the information will only be available if you record all of your money transactions.

It is important to know how your business is doing at any one time so that you know you are on the right track. If you notice that your business accounts are not meeting targets you have set and that profits are not as high as you would like, perhaps you could go back to your clients and ask how improvements in your service could be made. The response may be that more services could be introduced; for example, leg waxing and perhaps different perms with a higher price range. This further market research would result in more choice and happier clients who are getting what *they* want. You would also gain satisfaction from hitting proposed targets. Remember, a business plan for the first year should be reviewed and changed accordingly to maintain profits.

5: Useful Addresses

AA (Automobile Association)
Fanum House
Basingstoke
Hants RG21 2EA
0800 919595

Access
The Joint Credit Card Co. Ltd
Chartwell House
365 Chartwell Square
Southend-on-Sea SS2 5ST
01702 352266

Advertising Association
Abford House
15 Wilton Road
London SW1V 1NJ
0171 828 2771

The Association of Independent Businesses
Stag House
37 Pembridge Villas
London W11 3EP
0171 329 0219

Babyliss (UK) Ltd
Prospect Place
Mill Lane
Alton
Hants GU34 2QB
0990 133191

Barclaycard
PO Box 444
Dickinson Street
Manchester
0161 953 5200

Charles Allison House
Yarm Road
Stockton-on-Tees TS18 3RZ
01642 344744

Belmont Salon Supplies Ltd
174 West End Lane
London NW6 1SD
0181 992 7708

The British Red Cross Society National Headquarters
London Branch Headquarters
26 Worple Road
London SW19
0181 944 8909

British Institute of Management
Management House
Cottingham Road
Corby
Northants NN17 1TT
01536 204222

Business Link (Head Office)
4 New Fields
Stinford Road
Nuffield
Poole
Dorset BH17 7NF
01345 448844

Capital Hair & Beauty Ltd
Unit 6
Sackville Trading Estate
Sackville Road
Hove
E. Sussex BN3 7AN
01273 327215

Comby (London) Ltd
9–10 Violet Hill
London NW8 9EB
0181 830 0234

Design Council
1 Oxenden Street
London SW1Y 4EE
0171 208 2121

Freelance Hair and Beauty Federation
1 Osmonde Close
Worthing
W. Sussex BN14 7AJ
01903 234863

Hair and Beauty Direct
Freepost BR1143
Hove
E. Sussex BN3 7XX
0800 435355

Hair Development (UK) Ltd
Hair Extensions and Toupees
245 Mile End Road
London E1 4BJ
0171 790 3996/4567

Ogee/Sally Hair & Beauty Supplies
Unit 4, Area 10
Headley Park Industrial Estate
Woodley
Reading RG5 4SW
01734 504501

Open University Associate Students
Central Office
PO Box 76
Milton Keynes MK3 5HW
01908 652007

Patent Office
Marketing and Information Directorate
The Patent Office
Cardiff Road
Newport
Gwent NP9 1RH
0645 500505

The Prince's Youth Business Trust
5 Cleveland Place
London SW1Y 6JJ
0171 321 6500

RAC Motoring Services
PO Box 700
Bristol
Avon BS99 1RB
0345 331133

Rural Development Commission
141 Castle Street
Salisbury
Wilts SP1 3TP
01722 336255

St John Ambulance National Headquarters
1 Grosvenor Crescent
London SW1X 7EF
0171 235 5231

Schwarzkopf Ltd
California Industrial Estate
Penn Road
Aylesbury
Bucks HP21 8HL
01296 314000

Smith's Hairdressing Wholesalers Ltd
201-205 Crystal Palace Road
London SE22 9EW
0181 693 1956

Index

Index

Index